4/11

Women *of Achievement*

Anita Roddick

Women of Achievement

Abigail Adams
Susan B. Anthony
Tyra Banks
Clara Barton
Hillary Rodham Clinton
Marie Curie
Ellen DeGeneres
Diana, Princess of Wales
Tina Fey
Ruth Bader Ginsburg
Joan of Arc
Helen Keller
Madonna
Michelle Obama
Sandra Day O'Connor
Georgia O'Keeffe
Nancy Pelosi
Rachael Ray
Anita Roddick
Eleanor Roosevelt
Martha Stewart
Barbara Walters
Venus and Serena Williams

Women of Achievement

Anita Roddick

ENTREPRENEUR

Sherry Beck Paprocki

CHELSEA HOUSE
PUBLISHERS
An imprint of Infobase Publishing

ANITA RODDICK

Chelsea House
An imprint of Infobase Publishing
132 West 31st Street
New York, NY 10001

Library of Congress Cataloging-in-Publication Data
Paprocki, Sherry Beck.
 Anita Roddick : entrepreneur / by Sherry Beck Paprocki.
 p. cm. — (Women of achievement)
 Includes bibliographical references and index.
 ISBN 978-1-60413-688-3 (hardcover)
 1. Roddick, Anita, 1942–2007—Juvenile literature. 2. Body Shop (Firm)—History—Juvenile literature. 3. Cosmetics industry—Great Britain—History—Juvenile literature. 4. Businesswomen—Great Britain—Biography. I. Title. II. Series.

 HD9970.5.C672R63 2010
 381'.4566855092—dc22
 [B]
                    2009052752

Chelsea House books are available at special discounts when purchased in bulk quantities for businesses, associations, institutions, or sales promotions. Please call our Special Sales Department in New York at (212) 967-8800 or (800) 322-8755.

You can find Chelsea House on the World Wide Web at http://www.chelseahouse.com.

Text design by Erik Lindstrom
Cover design by Ben Peterson
Composition by EJB Publishing Services
Cover printed by Bang Printing, Brainerd, Minn.
Book printed and bound by Bang Printing, Brainerd, Minn.
Date printed: September 2010
Printed in the United States of America
10 9 8 7 6 5 4 3 2 1

This book is printed on acid-free paper.

All links and Web addresses were checked and verified to be correct at the time of publication. Because of the dynamic nature of the Web, some addresses and links may have changed since publication and may no longer be valid.

CONTENTS

1	A Global Concern	7
2	Growing Up Entrepreneurial	16
3	Adventures with Gordon	27
4	The Body Shop Opens	35
5	Creating the Story	44
6	The Body Shop Goes Public	54
7	Being Green	69
8	Big Changes	81
	Chronology	97
	Notes	99
	Bibliography	107
	Further Resources	112
	Picture Credits	113
	Index	114
	About the Author	119

A Global Concern

The life and passions of Anita Roddick can be glimpsed on a single winter day in 1991. Roddick is darting around her office showing a reporter for *The Independent*, a newspaper based in London, England, the treasures that she has brought back from her travels. There is bark from trees in China, a large thistle from the rain forest, a seedpod from Africa, and more. "These are nightingales' droppings," she explains. "They don't smell that bad, do they?"[1]

This is Anita Roddick, the high-strung, quirky, and energetic founder of a multimillion-dollar company called The Body Shop, a business that she built on environmental principles and a global concern. Roddick is a dynamo of a woman, only 5 feet 2 inches tall, with ringlets of wild dark hair that encircle her face. Although other women who work in her company dress professionally, it is not unusual for Roddick to wear Bermuda shorts, a man's shirt, and no makeup. Anita Roddick has never felt a need to put on airs.

During this meeting, Roddick is so fidgety that she does not bother to sit down at her desk, despite repeated requests from the reporter that the two embark on a conversation. Instead, she goes from one thing to the next in her office, sharing the story of her business and touching the goods that her company is now producing. What started as a simple business concept for creating body lotion from natural products has grown into a multinational, multimillion-dollar corporation.

The company headquarters is situated down the road from where Roddick was born, in the town of Littlehampton, nearly an hour southwest of London on the southern shores of England. It is from here that The Body Shop has grown to include more than 2,000 locations in 49 countries.

Roddick's office has a huge bulletin board filled with postcards and newspaper clippings from her travels around England and the world. As she shares the large beans from the African tree, Roddick explains to the reporter that they can be sprayed with perfume and used as potpourri in The Body Shop stores.

Outside of her office, in The Body Shop's production facility, there is a long corridor where employees pass. Sometimes Roddick sees pencil marks along the wall where they drag their hands as they walk along the hall. Being the creative thinker that she always has been, this business entrepreneur comes up with a solution. "We need to build some sort of musical instrument into the wall so employees can play music," she tells another visiting reporter. Roddick thinks a built-in xylophone would solve the wall problem.[2]

Anita Roddick's mind, it seems, never stops working. She flits from one topic to the next. She talks about how her

Entrepreneur and activist Anita Roddick poses for a portrait in her clip-covered office at The Body Shop headquarters in Littlehampton, Sussex, England.

company is making paper from water hyacinths in Nepal. "We started using the water hyacinths that were blocking the rivers," she says.[3]

A SOCIAL ACTIVIST

By 1991, it is well known that Roddick, an environmentalist and social activist, has never missed an opportunity to use natural products in a way that can boost her business. She is credited with being one of the first business founders to pay attention to ecological concerns. Despite her innovative thinking, she struggled to build her first business in 1976. Because banks did not take her seriously when she asked for loans, she had to take along her husband to convince them. But she stuck with her unique set of principles and built a business that would eventually be worth more than a billion dollars.[4]

Roddick built a huge business partly by traveling the world and collecting resources that would help create unique products. "I was constantly on the lookout for new ideas and new products, no matter how quirky they seemed at first," she wrote in her book *Body and Soul.* In fact, she once bought a secret family recipe for a skin-care treatment from a woman who traveled from Vienna and showed up at Roddick's office with a proposal.[5]

Before she opened her first store, Roddick spent many years thinking about the natural ingredients that women she had met in different countries used to soften their skin. One of these ingredients was cocoa butter, to which women in Tahiti introduced her. The women shared their biggest beauty secret—that cocoa butter kept their skin soft and fresh. That became one of the first products that Roddick introduced at The Body Shop. Soon thereafter, she hired an herbalist to create other products offered by the store, ones that included cocoa butter, aloe vera, almond oil, and other unique ingredients not being used in the cosmetics industry at that time.[6]

LEARNING ABOUT OTHER CULTURES

Although she runs a multinational company, Roddick continues to travel, always packing her suitcase for places such as Brazil and Nepal in her search for more natural oils from odd sorts of nuts, muds from unique geographical terrains, and cleansing techniques practiced by various cultures.

Her love of traveling started back in her teen years: once she took two months to hitchhike around Israel, and later she worked at the United Nations in Switzerland. It was then, perhaps, that she was infused with a wanderlust that would take her on many more travels. As a young woman, she traveled alone to Tahiti, Australia, and Africa before returning to the tiny town of Littlehampton.

During her interview on that day in 1991, Roddick notes that she has the freedom to travel throughout the world anytime she wants to do so. Instead of taking luxury trips like so many other wealthy people, she takes trips to poor countries where she can learn about other cultures and perhaps even help the people who live there. "The poverty was dreadful," she recalls, regarding her first trip to India. She still finds it difficult to visit places such as India, where people were begging and tugging on her shirtsleeves as they asked for money. Yet Roddick was fascinated by it all. "The sights and sounds and smells and colours were captivating," she says.[7]

Even when she travels, Roddick is a humanitarian. She always uses her problem-solving skills to try to help other people, including those who are less fortunate than herself. She has hundreds of ideas every day, and those ideas never stop, even when she is away from her office.

For example, Roddick's mind was working hard when she visited Boys Town during a trip to India. Roddick was awed by what surrounded her in the little white cottage where she was staying. She felt as if she was in paradise, surrounded by the beautiful pink and white flowers of rhododendron and azalea bushes.

Boys Town is a place where poor young men work to earn their living. During her visit, Roddick was deeply moved by the work ethic of the boys in the woodshop nearby—the boys there had created small wooden rollers that she could sell as foot massagers in The Body Shop. Before she left, Roddick placed an order for hundreds of the massagers. She was thrilled that she was helping to improve the lives of these poor youngsters, as well as coming up with a new product for her company to sell.[8]

In 1991, Roddick is a strong advocate for change. She shows that she cares about people and wants them to like their work. When she hires people, it is more important to her that they are enthusiastic and creative than that they have the right college degree or other credentials. She gives her workers a half-day off each week so they can do service work in the community. She also tries to create a relaxed and fun environment at the office. "Work should be a playground, an inspiration, an esthetic thing, not a Monday-to-Friday sort of death," she says.[9]

Roddick puts people who want to buy franchises of The Body Shop through an unusual process, often involving long conversations about motherhood, the environment, homelessness, and other issues. Some franchisees say that they never really talk about cosmetics while they are being trained. The application for a franchise at The Body Shop requires that it be handwritten, and it asks odd questions,

IN HER OWN WORDS

In her book *Business as Unusual,* Anita Roddick recalls the exact point in her life that led to her activism:

> My personal capacity for moral outrage was stimulated when I was about 10 years old and I picked up a paperback book—one of those cheap editions that were just starting to get popular back in the 1950s. It was about the Holocaust. There were six pages of photographs from Auschwitz and they made such an impression on me that I can describe every one of them to this day. . . . From that day onward I became a shouter, a marcher, a teenage campaigner.

such as which countries you have visited, which books you have read, and how you would like to die.

Roddick even invites those who want to be in the business to visit the corporate headquarters and sometimes to visit her home. It is an unusual way of doing business, but she cares little for what anyone thinks. One woman who is buying a franchise says that meeting Roddick is like being hit by lightning.[10]

Roddick's personal passion, however, is working for social causes. She has already crusaded against testing cosmetics on animals and has worked with Greenpeace to protest hazardous waste in the North Sea. She also works on campaigns to save whales, to protest against acid rain, and to protect the ozone layer, as well as other environmental causes. She even has staff members who create posters for The Body Shop stores that celebrate other world causes.

As The Body Shop has become more successful, she sees greater opportunities for global activism and social responsibility. She has joined with her husband, Gordon, and a good friend to produce a magazine called *The Big Issue*, sold by homeless people throughout England. The proceeds from magazine sales help poor people get jobs and find places to live. As Roddick has become wealthier and more powerful, she has come to consider herself a social reformer—someone who can change the world.

Still, Roddick seems to create chaos and controversy wherever she goes. Once while visiting The Body Shop in Manhattan, she breezed through the store, admiring displays and talking with staff. She went unrecognized at first because she never wears a business suit, although some people expect her to. While in Manhattan on this day, she wore a baggy white sweatshirt, sweatpants, and sneakers. In the store, she made suggestions that sounded nearly like commands. She ordered the store managers to get rid of a tray of hair clips that she considers tacky. Then, in a meeting with managers, she prodded them about what makes them angry.

CHALLENGING HER EMPLOYEES

As a business owner, Roddick challenges her employees to initiate discussions with her and improve business operations. Some find her hard to keep up with, however, complaining that though she cares about people, she rarely spends any time connecting with them. She likes people who listen to her but often does not take the time to listen to others. It is an accurate assessment: she is charming and excitable and lovable and funny, but rarely does she let anyone else do much of the talking.

Certainly, not everyone loves Anita Roddick's style. Some employees have called her a dictator; others have railed against her constant entreaties to remain energetic, spontaneous, and creative. Even a writer who is helping her with her books is struck by her inability to slow down and is forced to travel with her on airplanes so that he can do interviews. "She needed to sit down and talk to me about her life—and Anita never sat down," explained the writer. "If I remember correctly there were no chairs in her large office at The Body Shop."[11]

In interviews, she admits that she rarely sleeps much at night and implies that her lack of rest has led to her somewhat rash leadership qualities: She is often impolite, undiplomatic, and impatient with other people. She is continually looking for the next move she will make, both in business and in social activism. Her business life and her personal life, it seems, are tightly intertwined. But she never regrets it.

Journalists who interview her sometimes complain that she does not answer their questions and even that she saps energy out of a room. "It is Anita who controls the most controversial part of The Body Shop ethos—what she would call 'education' and I would call 'sermonising,'" wrote one journalist for *The Independent*. "You will never just go into a Body Shop and buy some soap; you will always be confronted with a poster or pamphlet or even a shop assistant banging on about the need to save the whale or the rainforest."[12]

Nonetheless, it is this type of activism that keeps Anita Roddick engaged in her business. As the company grows beyond a small, entrepreneurial concern into a large, public entity, she is challenged to keep an aging business functioning like a young one. In 1991, the Body Shop is 15 years old, and Roddick is still passionate about it. A tireless leader who has never stopped thinking about the next step for her business or the next campaign for the environment or for humanity, she has become one of Great Britain's leading business minds, a woman who has built an empire on products used mainly by other women.

How did Anita Roddick become such a successful businesswoman? Not for a love of money. Born the third of four children to Italian immigrants, she always had a strong work ethic. And it is in her youth that we can discover how her life was greatly influenced by hard work and the grit of earning a living.

Growing Up
Entrepreneurial

Anita Lucia Perilli was born on October 23, 1942, the child of Italian immigrants who ran a restaurant on the southern coast of England, in a small city in West Sussex. English residents from all around the country visited Littlehampton during the summer season and were served by many of Anita's relatives who owned restaurants and cafés.

The family restaurant, the Clifton Café, served hamburgers and other American fare. Because the Perillis were a big Italian family that laughed and talked loudly, Anita felt that she was different from many of the English families in Littlehampton, who were far less boisterous. She sometimes joked that others in the community never smelled garlic—which her parents and her Italian relatives used often in their cooking—before her family arrived in Littlehampton.

Roddick's mother, Gilda, had arrived in Great Britain many years before Anita was born, moving from a small village in Italy to become an English nanny at the age of 15.[1] Donny, the man whom Anita thought was her father, also immigrated to England at a very young age.

AN ARRANGED MARRIAGE

Gilda and Donny's old fashioned parents had arranged their children's marriage in Italy, agreeing that the couple would wed each other once they arrived in England. After marrying Donny, Anita's mother first gave birth to two daughters named Lydia and Velia. Then, a few years later, she had Anita and her younger brother, Bruno. Anita's mother and father eventually divorced.

After the divorce, Anita was surprised to learn that Donny Perilli was not her real father. It had taken Gilda many years to get the courage to divorce her husband from the arranged marriage so that she could marry the man she truly loved, Donny's cousin Henry, who had just returned from many years in America.

Henry purchased the Clifton Café from Donny and began expanding the restaurant's menu to include Coca-Cola and other treats that were unfamiliar in the United Kingdom at the time. He added bright colors and a jukebox, as well as other aesthetic touches he had learned in America.

Anita discovered that Henry was her biological father when she was about 19 years old. Gilda had married Henry after her divorce from Donny, but Henry died from tuberculosis only 18 months after their marriage. One day, while brushing her hair, Anita remarked to her mother that it was sad that Gilda and Henry had not ever had children together. That was when she learned the truth: Henry was not only Anita's father, but also Bruno's. Gilda had given birth to another man's children while she was married to

Donny.[2] "I will never forget the absolute joy of that moment when I learned that the man who I had always thought was my stepfather—and whom I adored—was actually my real father," wrote Roddick in her book *Body and Soul*.[3] Her older sisters learned the truth many years later, as adults. "It all makes sense," they told her. "Why you look different to us and how crazy you are!"[4]

After Henry died, Anita saw that her mother had to work very hard in the Clifton Café in order to raise her family. Anita and her siblings worked hard, too. They took orders, cleared tables, and washed dishes as soon as they were old enough to help out. The Clifton Café had long hours, opening for breakfast at 5 A.M. and not closing until the last customer of the day was gone. Years later, Roddick recalled knowing at a young age that she did not want to work in her mother's restaurant for the rest of her life. "All entrepreneurs share a sense of loss," she once told a reporter. "That's why they are driven."[5]

When not working, Anita attended a school at St. Catherine's Convent, where many nuns were her teachers. She began her first tiny business venture while she was there, trading comics from the American papers that Henry had brought back from America. The English children were excited to get American goods, which included bubblegum and other small surprises. Meanwhile, Anita was happy to trade for things such as cigarette cards, which were packed in cartons of cigarettes to make the boxes stiffer and to advertise the brand.

During her time at St. Catherine's, Anita met a nun who made a big impression on her. "I was so carried away by her innate goodness that I gave my new school uniform to another girl from a very poor family," Anita wrote some years later.[6] This act of giving would be but the first step on her road to social activism. It was the discovery of a book about the Holocaust when she was 10 years old that sealed her enthusiasm for helping others.

After finishing at St. Catherine's, she went to another nearby school, the Maude Allen Secondary Modern School for Girls. There, she studied drama and enjoyed the poetry of Walt Whitman, among other great writers. She was a huge fan of actor James Dean, who despite starring in just three movies, made an enormous impact on Anita. In fact, she was so affected by Dean's acting that she once performed a solo act in her school's talent competition in which she dressed in black, was bound with chains, and began her performance with a loud scream.

Despite working at her mother's restaurant after school, Anita also had a lot of fun as a teenager. She often went to a local amusement park and danced at the Top Hat ballroom. The influence of the nun she knew in elementary school seemed to stay with her; she was part of many social movements in the 1960s, including a group called Shelter and Freedom from Hunger. "You name it—we protested about everything," she recalled.[7] As a teenager, she also marched with the Campaign for Nuclear Disarmament and protested with a group called Campaign for Freedom Against Hunger.

AFTER HIGH SCHOOL

Despite her activism, Anita was not the most focused of students. She failed to get into the Central School of Speech and Drama (now part of the University of London) but was offered a position at the Guildhall School of Music and Drama.[8] With her mother's encouragement, she instead chose the Newton Park College of Education in Bath, England.[9] It is there that she learned about art and design, an education that would aid her later in life as she developed the prototypes for The Body Shop.

On April 19, 1965, thousands of people fill Trafalgar Square in London, England, for a huge rally marking the end of a three-day "Easter March for Peace" organized by the Campaign for Nuclear Disarmament, a group with which Anita Roddick was associated at the time.

While Anita was studying at Newton, her mother sold the Clifton Café and opened a lively nightclub in Littlehampton called El Cubana. Gilda, quite the character, dressed in sparkling gowns every night and sat at the bar all evening, smoking and telling jokes in her raspy Italian accent. As her mother turned El Cubana into a rousing hangout, Anita learned another lesson about business.

GOING ON KIBBUTZ

While at Newton, Anita won a three-month scholarship to study on a kibbutz in Israel in order to write her senior thesis—a long paper necessary to complete her degree—which she titled "The Children of the Kibbutz."[10] That trip changed her life in many ways. Anita, whose mother always told her that she had some Jewish heritage, became intent on learning as much as she could about Israel and Judaism during the trip. She did a lot of physical labor during her stay, arising at 3 A.M. to work in the fields or to go out on fishing boats. "I learned there was nothing more important in life than love and work," she said.[11]

Her stay on the kibbutz, however, ended badly. One day she made a joke about a friend walking on water as he waded out into the ocean. The next morning, both she and her friend were asked by the elders of the kibbutz to leave. She spent the next few months hitchhiking around Israel and had many experiences while moving around the country.

When she eventually returned to England, she wanted to convert to Judaism. A rabbi she visited, though, thought she had too much of a romantic notion of the culture and talked her out of the conversion. Still, she later realized that the trip had aided her in other ways, in particular by convincing her that she was capable and independent enough to travel alone anywhere in the world. Throughout her life, that would become a huge asset as she built her business at The Body Shop.

Once Anita finished her coursework at Newton, she applied for and was given a teaching job at a junior school nearby. But when a friend invited her to visit him in Paris a few weeks before school began, she could not turn him down. Before long, her love of adventure and traveling to new places convinced her that she should stay in Paris longer than just a few days. She resigned from the teaching position that she had not yet started and stayed. In Paris, she filled her time by meeting writers, artists, and musicians, and she visited local jazz clubs in the evenings. To support herself, she got a job clipping articles for the *International Herald Tribune*.[12]

WHAT IS A KIBBUTZ?

A kibbutz is a commune in Israel where people live and work together to form a community that is dependent on all of its members. It is estimated that there are approximately 270 kibbutzim in Israel with nearly 120,000 people living on them.[*]

The first kibbutz, Degania, was established in 1909, with land that was acquired by the National Jewish Fund. Degania, which is derived from a Hebrew word meaning grain, was primarily an agricultural commune, as were most kibbutzim that have been founded through the years.

Jewish people of all ages live on a kibbutz. Each adult or family has their own living quarters and gardens, and their children live with them until high school, when they attend school with children from other kibbutzim. Children who grow up on a kibbutz understand that everyone, including themselves, must work together to make the community operate efficiently. The community works together to farm the land and to raise animals. Today, some kibbutzim include other industries outside of agriculture, such as manufacturing metals, plastics, foods, and clothing.

Members of a kibbutz are assigned jobs within the community, such as working in the kitchen or the dining hall. An elected administrator heads up the economic group and a new person is put into this position every two to three years.

After nearly a year, however, Anita was ready to move on. She returned to Littlehampton to begin teaching at the school she had once attended, the Maude Allen Secondary Modern School for Girls. It was only a part-time position, but she later got work as a full-time teacher in nearby

As many as 600 people can live together on a kibbutz. Residents rule the kibbutz in committees and share a dining hall, an auditorium, a library, a swimming pool, tennis courts, a medical clinic, and a grocery store, among other facilities. Because Israel has grown, some kibbutzim are now suburbs of cities and provide services to local residents, such as catering and laundry services. Some members work outside of the kibbutz, but if they do so, then they must turn over their earnings to the community.

Life on the kibbutz can be very busy. There is a lot to do, on top of working and playing. Each community has unique customs and celebrations for Jewish holidays, Israeli holidays, and family ceremonies such as weddings and bar/bat mitzvahs. Agricultural events, some of which have been recognized since biblical times, are commemorated with singing and dancing.

Because the kibbutzim have become more interesting to tourists and college students, some now offer recreational facilities such as guesthouses, swimming pools, horseback riding, exotic animal farms, and more.

* "The Kibbutz," Jewish Virtual Library, http://www. jewishvirtuallibrary.org.

During her youthful travels, Anita Roddick lived briefly on a kibbutz in Israel. Here, members build a mud-brick house on the Yael Negev kibbutz in Israel.

Southampton. "I set out to make my classroom the most enthralling place in the world," she wrote in her book *Body and Soul*. "I would move all the desks and chairs into the center, put up brilliant graphics all round the walls and invite the kids to walk around and make notes."[13]

After her first year of teaching, she decided to visit Greece all alone. On the way back home, she stopped in Geneva, Switzerland, where she used her best persuasive skills to land a job at the United Nations (UN). She worked for the International Labour Organization at the UN for the following year, helping to organize conferences for experts to discuss the needs of women in developing countries. After several months, however, she found it horribly ironic that officials at the UN would eat huge meals while discussing the problems of the third world, where many people went hungry. Once again, she was ready to move on.

TRAVELING THE HIPPIE TRAIL

At this point in her young life, she began her journey on the so-called Hippie Trail. The Hippie Trail was a movement in the 1960s and early 1970s by young people who wanted to explore the world. Many of them started in Europe and traveled to the Middle East and Africa, either alone or with small groups of friends. Some hitchhiked much of the way; others took trains or buses.

Anita traveled alone, taking a boat to Tahiti. She thought Tahiti would be the most exotic place she could visit, sailing through the Panama Canal to get there. After

IN HER OWN WORDS

While traveling in apartheid-era South Africa, Anita Roddick decided to see what would happen if she attended a black-only night at a jazz club in Johannesburg. The following are her thoughts, published many years later in her book *Body and Soul*:

> In Johannesburg I got into trouble by going to a club on the wrong night. It was one of those places which had alternate nights for different races, but I didn't want to hear black jazz with a lot of white racists, so I went on a "black night."

a month in Tahiti, she sailed for Australia. While there, she began selling wooden siding—which were boards used on the outside of homes—in order to continue financing her travels. By this point, she had a lot of confidence in her ability to sell things to people, and she also loved getting to know her customers.

After visiting several cities in Australia, she went to Madagascar and then to South Africa. Between 1948 and 1994, the minority white government maintained the system of apartheid in South Africa—a formal racial segregation system that barred black and white people from interacting with one another. People were arrested if they broke these segregation laws. Anita did not believe that people should be kept apart just because of the color of their skin. But she did not realize the trouble she would get into if she went to a jazz club on a night when only black people were allowed to attend.

"Of course, I was picked up almost immediately by the police and given twenty-four hours to get out of the country," she recalled years later in *Body and Soul*.[14] (It was not until many years after her trip to South Africa that the apartheid government finally ended. By 1994, the system of apartheid had been abolished and Nelson Mandela was elected South Africa's first black president.) Having little choice, she decided to head home to Littlehampton. What Anita did not know was that her mother had someone waiting to meet her back at El Cubana.

Adventures
with Gordon

While Anita Perilli was globetrotting around the world, she had little knowledge about what was happening in Littlehampton. In the late 1960s, long before the Internet was invented, it sometimes took days or weeks for personal correspondence, in the form of letters or postcards, to be received internationally. When faster communications occurred, they were in the form of telegrams or telephone calls, but people used those less frequently because they were expensive.

When Anita arrived back in Littlehampton, her mother had a surprise awaiting her at El Cubana. On her first night home, she was introduced to a tall and handsome Scotsman named Gordon Roddick. "The moment I set eyes on Gordon Roddick in the El Cubana I knew that I wanted him to be the father of my children," she wrote in her book *Body and Soul*.[1] Gordon later recalled to a reporter: "I fell in love with her as soon as I saw her and I knew my previous life was over."[2]

Even though they fell for each other quickly, they could not have been more opposite: While she was talkative and vivacious, he was quiet and observational. Anita was trained as a teacher, but Gordon wanted to be a writer and was working on a local farm while he wrote children's stories. But they had some important things in common. Like Anita, Gordon had traveled to various countries. They soon discovered that they had, at different times, even lived on the same street in Sydney, Australia, and knew many of the same people.[3] Because Gordon had arrived in Littlehampton six months before Anita went home, he had been reading about her travels in the postcards and letters that her mother hung up behind the bar at El Cubana. When they were finally introduced, Gordon felt like he already knew her.

AN INSTANT RAPPORT

"We had an instant rapport," Anita Roddick later explained, "even though our only shared experience was that we both

DID YOU KNOW?

Anita Roddick was always an adventurer. Her early travels around the world led her to create some surprise formulas for lotions later sold by The Body Shop. Among them were many products made with cocoa butter. Women in Tahiti had demonstrated how they used the butter, rubbing it on their bodies as they had been taught by their mothers and grandmothers to keep their skin smooth.

spent quite a bit of time traveling the world."[4] Anita and Gordon were both 26 years old and were fascinated by what the future would bring them.[5]

Perhaps Anita's friendly mother and her large Italian family made Gordon feel welcome in Littlehampton. Both of Gordon Roddick's parents had died by the time he was seven years old. When he was four, his father, who had been a grain broker, died of liver disease. Three years later, Gordon's mother died of a brain hemorrhage. Young Gordon was sent away to boarding school and visited aunts and uncles during holidays. "It made me very independent," Gordon said years later. Upon graduating, Gordon worked in tin mines in Australia and on ranches in Latin America and in Africa.[6]

It may have seemed to Gordon that when he arrived in Littlehampton, he also had arrived home. Within five days after Anita returned, she and Gordon seemed inseparable. She moved into Gordon's rented flat and again took a teaching job. The two of them often discussed owning a business together, too. Sometimes they talked about moving to Australia and starting a pineapple plantation.

But their plans were stalled when Anita discovered that she was pregnant. After their daughter Justine was born, Gordon worked hard trying to earn more money to support his young family. But, still, he and Anita talked seriously about opening their own business.

Justine was only 15 months old when Anita found that she was pregnant again. Before this baby would be born, though, Anita and Gordon decided to take a big trip together. They planned a vacation to the United States to visit friends in San Francisco. "We were supposed to be looking for business opportunities, but were actually just having a good time," explained Anita, in her book *Business as Unusual.*[7]

Many years later, a reporter for a London newspaper claimed that the couple visited two small, eclectic shops

A shopping precinct in Littlehampton, West Sussex, England, Anita Roddick's hometown.

while in San Francisco and Berkeley, California, that featured biodegradable shampoos and lotions that were made with avocado, cocoa butter, and other natural ingredients. The reporter claimed that Anita had copied the shops' concept and even borrowed the name when she opened her own shop six years later. The shops in California eventually were renamed Body Time, although they had originally been called The Body Shop. The reporter wrote that the Roddicks had purchased the concept in a deal that was supposed to be kept secret.[8]

The trip to the United States was important in a more personal way to Anita and Gordon. While taking little

Justine on a drive with them to Reno, Nevada, the two decided that they would finally get married. During the ceremony, a very pregnant Anita wore a pair of corduroy slacks and a red rain jacket, and Justine was strapped in a pouch on her back. The wedding ceremony took less than a minute and cost them $25. Afterward, Anita placed a long distance call to her mother in England to announce the news. Later that day, the three Roddicks joined their two California friends in a cheap hotel for the night.[9]

STARTING A BUSINESS

Their second daughter, Samantha, was born a few months later in England. It was 1971 and Gordon and Anita were still talking about their next adventure. A restless person by nature, she brainstormed new ideas with Gordon while caring for her two little girls.

Together, Anita and Gordon decided that they would buy a run-down Victorian residential hotel, named St Winifred's, in the middle of Littlehampton. The two Roddicks agreed that they would repair the eight-bedroom building and turn it into a charming bed and breakfast inn.[10] "Gordon and I had always wanted to find a way in which we could work together, and making our home into our business meant we could even divide up domestic responsibilities like looking after the children," said Roddick.[11] The situation seemed ideal.

After one busy summer season, however, the Roddicks recognized a flaw in their plan. Business at the inn nearly came to a halt once the tourist season was over. The couple feared they would go bankrupt. The huge Victorian building was expensive to heat and maintain, so they quickly decided to rent many of its rooms on a long-term basis, once again turning St Winifred's into a residential hotel. Soon, the hotel was filled with tenants, including several elderly folks who had interesting personalities. "At Justine's third birthday party, another guest walked into the room in a silk housecoat and threw a bucket of water over the assembled mothers," Anita reported years later.[12]

Nonetheless, their elderly residents had helped stabilize their hotel business. With St Winifred's making a small profit, the Roddicks started making more business plans. They rented space in a nearby building and opened a restaurant called Paddington's, where they planned to feature healthy dishes such as soups and quiches. After spending so many years in her family's restaurant business, Anita thought this venture would be a huge success. Although such food is popular today, people in Littlehampton were not interested in such dishes. "It was a disaster," Anita Roddick later wrote. "No one seemed to share our enthusiasm for the menu."[13]

A CHANGE IN PLANS

The experience allowed the Roddicks to realize how important it was to provide a service that their customers wanted. If the tourists and local residents did not want healthy food, perhaps there was another answer. Gordon had a brainstorm—they would turn the restaurant into a burger-and-fry place that played loud rock-and-roll music. After three weeks of sitting nearly empty, Paddington's quickly filled up and became one of the most popular hangouts in Littlehampton.[14]

Years later, Anita Roddick would marvel over the lessons she learned about business while she and her husband owned Paddington's. The husband-and-wife team learned to work well together, as well as to appreciate each other's differences. Gordon's quiet demeanor worked well with the staff, and his orderly personality kept the kitchen in good shape. Anita, on the other hand, made the perfect front person, with her vivacious personality and friendly smile making customers feel welcome and at home.

Still, the Roddicks learned firsthand that owning a restaurant was a difficult business. They had little time for themselves and for their young family. Anita and Gordon agreed that being socially conscious was important to them, but their contributions were limited to local issues. Sometimes Gordon would write messages on the blackboard at the restaurant about issues on which he disagreed with the city council. On occasion, they would organize a protest, such as one that encouraged the city to use empty building space to house the homeless. But beyond that, the Roddicks had little time or energy to be involved in their community.

Even though Anita Roddick knew how hard her mother had worked to run the Clifton Café, she and Gordon had no idea about the number of hours that would be required each week to run their restaurant. They wanted their own business so they could spend more time with their daughters. But that was not happening. In fact, they were home so infrequently that Anita's mother sold El Cubana and spent much of her time babysitting her young granddaughters, who were then six and four years old.

IN HER OWN WORDS

Roddick wrote about the experience of running Paddington's restaurant in Littlehampton with her husband in her book *Body and Soul*:

> We were rarely home before one o'clock in the morning and were often so tired we could hardly drag ourselves up the stairs to bed. Sometimes we would wake up the next day with our muscles aching so much that we could hardly get up.

After three years of owning Paddington's, Anita and Gordon were growing disheartened. They were earning barely enough money to pay for their needs and were exhausted each night when they dropped into bed. Their daughters saw more of Anita's mother than they did of their own. Late one night, as they were falling asleep, Gordon suggested they sell their restaurant business and begin a new adventure.

Anita did not argue. She was a person who constantly needed to explore new things and new ideas. She knew that a good leader needed to be assertive, curious, and willing to learn from experiences. As a young adult, Anita was discovering that her own experiences in business would help her become a better leader in the future.[15]

The Body Shop Opens

Anita Roddick was surprised. After deciding to sell Paddington's, her husband announced that he wanted to ride a horse from Buenos Aires, Argentina, to New York City. The trip would likely take two years.

In order for Gordon to pursue his childhood dream, he would need to leave Anita in England alone with their two young daughters. "I can't pretend I was thrilled at the prospect of him going off for two years and leaving the children and me," she said later, "but at the same time I could not help but admire him. It was such a romantic and brave thing to do that it was impossible to be resentful about it."[1]

Even though some of their friends were perplexed about his upcoming trip, with many thinking Anita and Gordon might divorce, Anita was not worried. The Roddicks were extremely independent. They each had dreams and ideas that they wanted to pursue, and they were reluctant to hold each other back. In fact, Anita was infatuated with the idea of Gordon's journey. "It blissed me out to have a partner that said, 'I've got to do this. I've got to be remarkable,'" Roddick later said.[2]

Still, Anita needed to figure out how she could earn a living for herself and her young daughters while Gordon was gone. As Gordon made plans for his trip, she began thinking about opening a store that would sell lotions and bath products. She wanted to be able to sell such items in small bottles, instead of forcing customers to pay for huge containers that were never used after the lotion was gone. She also thought it was important that these simple little bottles and jars could be reused; customers would bring the same containers back to the stores to refill them.

IDENTIFYING A NEED

"One of the great challenges for entrepreneurs is to identify a simple need," Roddick later wrote.[3] At the time, however, her passion for starting something new far outweighed her environmental consciousness. During the time that she was simply developing the concept for The Body Shop, she was only concerned about a few things: she needed to earn money for her family and knew she would have to work very hard at whatever she chose to do.

Even though she thought she had a great idea, Roddick encountered a few challenges along the way to opening her first store. First, she needed to get a loan from a bank for about £4,000, which equaled about $7,900, to help finance her endeavor. So, in jeans and a T-shirt, she went to her bank, with her two young children in tow. She and Gordon still owned and lived at St Winifred's, so she thought that the bank would be able to use their large house, with its significant worth as a multiunit rental property, as collateral for the loan. After exuberantly describing her idea for her business and talking nonstop about the natural products that were being used by women in other parts of the world, she was immediately turned down. The bank manager was completely unimpressed.

Anita was crushed and nearly ready to give up on her idea. She went home to tell Gordon, who was still planning his trip. His focused thoughts helped her understand what she had done wrong. Gordon suggested that Anita go out and buy a business suit. They also decided to ask a friend to help them put together an official business plan. Days later, Gordon went back to the bank with Anita and left the children at home with a sitter.

Immediately, their loan was approved. Anita Roddick was surprised to find out how important it was to be well dressed and have a prepared business plan. She had thought going to the bank with her wonderful idea and talking about all of the natural ingredients she had discovered on her travels around the world would be enough.

MAKING NATURAL PRODUCTS

Once their loan was approved, Anita Roddick got busy creating products from natural ingredients and trying them out, making a mess in her kitchen at home. She had trouble getting some of the solutions to work right, and finally she realized that she could use some help. Once again, she discovered that she could not do all of this work alone. She approached a few cosmetics companies and asked if they would be willing to create small amounts of products from natural ingredients, such as Rhassoul mud from Africa. "I think they thought I was completely mad," she recalled.[4]

After realizing that she would get no help from the cosmetics factories, Roddick found a young herbalist in the telephone book. She gave him a call and scheduled a meeting. He agreed that he could help her make about 25 products to start the store, from ingredients that included cocoa butter, jojoba oil, almond oil, and other natural ingredients. She paid him about $1,400 to get started.

Meanwhile, Roddick came to realize that Littlehampton was not the kind of town where a lotion store would work, so she started walking around the nearby town of Brighton to look for an empty shop. Finally, she found a dingy but inexpensive storefront. It was in fairly bad shape: it leaked when it rained, and moldy spots covered the walls.

Repairs were quickly made, however, and Roddick decided that green paint would cover the moldy splotches that were still on the walls. Somehow, that decision led to the color green being used as part of The Body Shop stores that would be opening in years to come. Of course, at the time, Roddick had no idea that there would be more stores in her future.

By now, Gordon was ready for his trip to Buenos Aires, and Anita was getting a little more nervous about her new idea. As they talked about her budget, he pointed out that she needed to earn about $600 a week to make it work. Anita hesitated, unsure if she could succeed. Gordon encouraged her to spend six months working at it, and if the store did not take off, he suggested that she and their daughters meet him in Peru.[5]

So Anita moved forward. Gordon was still in Littlehampton when she opened her first store in the Kensington Gardens neighborhood of Brighton on March 26, 1976. She was so busy by noon that she called him to help. By the end of the day, they had earned £130. Anita was thrilled. Perhaps, she thought, her plan would work.

ON HER OWN

About two months after the shop opened, Gordon left for Buenos Aires and Anita was on her own. She hired her first helper, a young woman who was 16 years old at the time. Many years later, the woman would report about her impressions of Roddick while helping her in that very first store. "She was inspirational and scary, like no one I had ever met before," she wrote.[6]

Each day, The Body Shop store would open in this edgy area of Brighton, near the town's clock tower and a big record store. The desirable store atmosphere that Anita created attracted streams of customers. The store had its green walls, small jars and bottles of lotions neatly stacked on shelves, and rock-and-roll music playing in the background. Anita and her young employee handwrote the labels and descriptions of what was contained in each product. Eventually, they started combining various bottles and jars into bigger baskets, purchased from a store down the street, and covering them in plastic. They used a hair dryer to shrink the plastic around the shape of the basket to create eye-appealing gifts, too. Soon, The Body Shop was selling not only individual bottles and jars of lotions, but also what Anita called "Beauty Baskets."[7] The new shop was such a hit that the local newspaper, the *Evening Argus*, published an article talking about Roddick's concept and her environmental values.[8]

One morning, Roddick showed up at the store with a recipe to make a body scrub out of wheat germ and oatmeal. She sent her young employee to a nearby health food shop to buy the ingredients and then directed her to the basement of The Body Shop, where the teenager ground the ingredients in a small food processor, mixed them together, and put them in small brown jars to sell in the shop upstairs. Roddick added this and other products, such as Honey and Oatmeal Scrub Mask, Cucumber Cleansing Milk, and Seaweed and Birch Shampoo, to her line of offerings.

NEW PRODUCTS AND SERVICES

This was a time before cosmetics companies were concerned about skin cancer, and none were yet including sunscreen ingredients in their lotions. Roddick created such a product by simply mixing cooking oil with some other products. She called it suntan lotion, and it sold well in the shop, too, even though it also did not include sunscreen.

Interestingly, Roddick decided not to add scents to her lotions because it was expensive to buy the perfumes. Instead, she set up a small perfume bar in her shop and encouraged her customers to add the scent of their choice to their product before they left the store.[9] Adding scent was another new idea, but again it was used only because Roddick was on a very tight budget. Her creativity never seemed to end. To lure customers, she often took the perfumes outside and squirted a path to her store.[10] She added bouquets of potpourri inside the shop, too, for a more fragrant essence.

Even though The Body Shop was already successful and had a lot of returning customers, Roddick wanted to add new services. One day she brought in an ear-piercing gun, which she had purchased elsewhere, and began offering that service to her customers as well. The new store owner was happy and very motivated by her company's early successes. Her friends stopped by often, and she loved visiting with them. She also made many new friends among her regular customers, because she loved meeting new people and talking about her products. She even loaded up her small, green van with lotions and set off in the evenings to talk to groups at schools and other places as a way to introduce them to her products. Roddick found that she was so busy that she once again depended on her mother to babysit for her daughters.

Her enthusiasm propelled her. Before long, Roddick had what she thought was another great idea: She would open another shop just up the road in a little town named Chichester. After a few weeks of searching for a site, she came up with a storefront that was slightly bigger than the store in Brighton. Even though the first shop was only a few months old, Roddick was sure the time was right for a second one.

A SECOND STORE

But, once again, the bank manager stalled her. He told her that she needed to wait a year before expanding her business. Although she was crushed, Roddick disagreed with the bank manager and refused to let go of the idea. Eventually, a friend named Aidre, who sometimes worked at the store, suggested that Roddick ask her boyfriend, Ian McGlinn, who owned a local automobile garage, for a loan.

McGlinn agreed to a deal: he would loan Anita the money she needed for her second shop if she agreed to sign a contract saying that he would be half owner of the whole business. Roddick agreed. In the years to come, many others would say that this was Anita Roddick's biggest business mistake.[11] Nonetheless, she quickly moved forward with McGlinn's money. Roddick and her friend Aidre worked together to open the second shop in Chichester. The two celebrated together, too, when both shops earned £100 in one day selling Christmas baskets.

LETTUCE LOTION AND MORE

Weeks later, Roddick was excited to hear from a young man named Mark Constantine, who was an herbalist interested in working with her. After the introduction of her first products, Roddick had not worked much with the original herbalist. Together, she worked with Constantine to perfect ideas that he brought to her. There was a lettuce lotion that originally had bits of lettuce floating in it, a honey and beeswax cleanser that originally had black specks floating in

Anita Roddick, chief executive of The Body Shop chain, is photographed in one of her stores in 1986. From the chain's earliest days, it sold all-natural toiletries and cosmetics manufactured without animal testing.

it, and other such products. Roddick gave Constantine the input he needed to make his creations more visually accept-able to the public. Their partnership would last for several years, with Constantine's small company growing along with The Body Shop's business.

With her undying passion for her business, Roddick con-tinued working nonstop. She began thinking about expan-sion again and now had customers who wanted to duplicate what she was offering. Requests came quickly from people who asked permission to open similar stores, agreeing to buy the products that The Body Shop produced.

At first, Roddick thought that would be a perfect arrangement. She knew that she would still make money if these stores sold her products. But creating and bottling the lotions and creams took a huge amount of work. Roddick knew a new plan was needed if she was going to permit others to open The Body Shop stores. Yet she was unsure of the answer.

Meanwhile, one of the horses that Gordon was using for his trip had died in Bolivia, so he decided to return to England. Just as Anita was trying to determine the best answers for expanding her business, Gordon came home. He had spent months on horseback, contemplating the wonderful potential of his wife's idea. Once back in England, Gordon and Anita met with an attorney and put together a formal franchising plan.

Within two years after Roddick had started her first store, The Body Shop expanded to include several locations in England, as well as the first one outside of that country: a kiosk in Brussels, Belgium. Anita Roddick was a very busy woman. She had a family and a handful of stores. And, when she had time, she still engaged in social causes that caught her eye. At various times, Roddick talked about the Quaker principles on which she tried to run her business. "[They] cared about their community, never paid themselves more than they needed to, and saw business as a community of peoples and the protection of other peoples," she explained. "They measured success in a different way."[12]

Like the Quakers, Roddick measured success differently. She never thought too far ahead about the business that she was building. She did not yet know that her vision would become one that millions of people would come to love. She did not know that she was on the cusp of building one of the world's most recognizable brands. And she had little reason to suspect that within 10 years she would become a very wealthy and very powerful woman.

Creating the Story

Although many other women were very successful at building empires in the cosmetics industry in the twentieth century, Anita Roddick had an unusual approach to business. While she initially forged her business to support her family, she was also driven by a passion for human and animal rights. It was that passion that would lead her to collect and retell the stories of the natural products that were sold at The Body Shop stores.

Like the Quakers to whom she frequently referred, she seemed less interested in making a huge profit. Yet the lives of people around the world were very important to her. For every product that Roddick sold, there was a story about where it came from and the people who used it. "When I arrived in Tahiti the first thing that struck me was the women," Roddick wrote in *Body and Soul*. "They had absolutely terrible teeth because they chewed sugar cane all the time, but their skin was like silk."[1]

Roddick finally got up the nerve to ask the women how they kept their skin so soft. "They showed me what looked like a lump of cold lard," she said. "It was . . . cocoa butter, extracted from cocoa pods, which they rubbed on their skins just as they had been taught by their mothers, and just as their mothers had been taught by their grandmothers."[2]

Many times through the years, Roddick would repeat such stories about her early travels and the trips she still took. These were the stories that helped make The Body Shop a big business. She often referred to those stories in her books, with reporters who interviewed her, and with her employees and customers, all in an effort to sell her products. Decades after she visited Tahiti, the story of cocoa butter even appeared on her Web site.

From the time she opened the first store, Roddick's stories were important to The Body Shop. They would be the stories that would make customers feel as though they were helping people in far-off lands, in addition to meeting their own needs for softer skin, when they bought the unusual body-care products.

WRITING SIMPLE NOTES

In the early days of The Body Shop, Roddick and her employees handwrote simple descriptions to accompany the lotions and shampoos that they sold. The notes explained things such as why there were black specks in the honey shampoos. (Roddick claimed the specks were from bees' feet.) The yarns, perhaps, were spun with truthfulness and a bit of imagination.

The refillable, inexpensive bottles that Roddick used for packaging helped add to The Body Shop's lore. The bottles gave customers a reason to believe that they were buying earth-friendly products. But the real reason that she used the small bottles was because they were cheap. Keeping down costs while promoting her products was the key to her early success. When she was starting her business in the 1970s, she also could not afford to advertise in newspapers, in magazines, or on television. But she knew how to express her passionate ideas to her employees and to her customers. She did not hesitate to encourage others to make a commitment to a better world. Roddick firmly believed that as a business leader she needed to be morally responsible. She once remarked, "The big question that none of us in business ever want to ask ourselves . . . is, does the growth of the business presuppose the destruction of the planet?"[3]

GETTING MEDIA ATTENTION

Partly because of her intense passion for creating a better world, Roddick never saw a need for advertising her stores in traditional ways, even after she had made millions of dollars that could have been spent on such campaigns. Instead, she knew that getting free media attention was as important to her business's growth as anything else. "That was Roddick's great genius," one British reporter wrote many years later.

> She wasn't really talking about moisturiser . . . She was using moisturiser to talk about human rights, and animal testing, and the environment. Moisturiser wasn't just a cream, it was politics— from the World Trade Organisation to the Nigerian Ogoni people—and it was big business.[4]

During her early years in business, Roddick had an eclectic, almost hippie-like attitude that she would take one day at a time and make that day be the best it could possibly be. As more shops opened and more employees were involved, she treated the business as an extended family. One of the first managers' meetings was held at her mother's house. Gilda cooked lasagna for all who attended.

As The Body Shop grew, Roddick realized that she was better at creating the stories that sold her products than anyone else she might pay to do the work. After a few years, however, she decided to hire a professional public relations person. That woman would help Roddick dream up stunts to get her product into the news more often. One such public relations campaign involved representatives from The Body Shop standing on the streets during a marathon, handing out small, free samples of Peppermint Foot Lotion to the runners as they passed by. "It was a cute little story that made many of the newspapers next day, and Peppermint Foot Lotion became one of our best sellers," Roddick said.[5]

When The Body Shop opened a store in London, the media became even more interested. The editors at major glossy magazines watched London's cosmopolitan shops and boutiques as they identified new trends. Soon after The Body Shop opened its first store in London, *Cosmopolitan* published a feature about it. This article sparked a media frenzy, with many magazines and television shows interested in Roddick and her ideas. When being interviewed, she wanted to talk about human rights but often had to endure doing silly things, such as the time during one television appearance that she created a natural face mask out of boiled lettuce and blended avocado. Nonetheless, Roddick knew that any appearance she made on television would help spread the word about The Body Shop.

All of this was a lot of fun. Gordon was now fully immersed in the business, and he and Anita enjoyed working together. They both had time to spend with their daughters,

Body Shop founder Anita Roddick is photographed with displays just out-side one of her stories in November 1982. Throughout her long career, Roddick used her international cosmetics chain to promote eco-friendly practices long before they were widely fashionable.

who were now school-aged, and they could afford to take nice vacations together as a family. While Anita visited shops and dreamed up new products, Gordon managed the company's growth. First, he rented an old furniture warehouse where the mixing, grinding, bottling, and labeling took place. Soon, though, The Body Shop outgrew that space, and the Roddicks convinced the banks to loan them money to build a larger warehouse, which also would soon become the company's headquarters. By now, shops were opening fast—at the rate of two a month—in countries that included Iceland, Denmark, Finland, and Holland.

Still, though, Roddick took one day at a time. "The first four or five years, when we were two or three, or five or ten shops, we never were interested in growth," she explained. "We were always interested in being counterculture. That was our absolute determination—we wanted to go into the opposite direction of everyone else."[6]

MAKING MISTAKES

Roddick made some mistakes along the way. One was allowing franchisees too much flexibility in the way their shops were run. At one time, shop managers were given the authority to veer away from the standard green interiors used by The Body Shop and were given the choice of using dark mahogany or stripped pine stains. After a few shops changed their interior designs, Roddick realized that she had made a mistake. The Body Shop's corporate green had been the best color to use all along.

As more shops opened, Roddick knew that the company needed to focus on its lotions, shampoos, and other such products. She had found that many of the stores were cluttered with knickknacks and other things. She soon helped managers and franchisees refocus on The Body Shop's main retail mission: selling unique body-care products made of natural ingredients.

Through all of this growth, Roddick remained a steadfast humanitarian. She was an advocate for free trade, which meant paying a fair price for products purchased from people and communities in poorer countries. She opposed testing cosmetics on animals, as other cosmetics companies were doing at the time. She believed in protecting human rights around the world and in protecting the planet's natural resources.

Roddick continued to influence people she met each day with her own concerns about the world. Perhaps because of her travels, she was an advocate for people in all parts of the world, and she surrounded herself with others who had similar feelings, both in her business and in her personal life. She deeply valued honesty, fairness, and respectfulness. Certainly, Roddick's business style was unconventional. Instead of being dedicated to building the best and most financially valuable business she could build, her focus was on building an honest and fair business that had a strong moral tone. "We never sat down and said, 'How can we be different,'" Roddick said. "A social commitment comes out of a belief in yourself, because as an entrepreneur what you're doing is putting out a thumbprint of who you are. Being the rabble-rouser that I am, I wanted my thumbprint on the canvas of The Body Shop."[7]

Roddick was also making her mark on the young people who worked with her. As The Body Shop expanded, she implored young employees to get involved in their communities. She nearly forced some of them to go to various protests while on their lunch hours. "It was impossible not to be in awe of this wild-haired woman who believed so hard in her hippy ideals," a reporter once wrote.[8] She held firm in her belief that employees should be a part of the community. "There's nothing more joyous in retailing," Roddick said, "than to engage in the community, to do volunteerism on company time."[9]

LEADERS SHOULD HAVE GOOD MORALS

Roddick was adamant that as a business leader, her concerns for human rights and for the entire the world would not be overlooked. "The leader has to have a moral agenda," she said. "If the leader is only saying we want to be the biggest or the most profitable company in the world, forget it."[10]

Despite her reasons for starting The Body Shop, this business leader had motives other than just making enough money to support her young family. Certainly, she was unique in her approach to business. The term "marketing" nearly repulsed her. Roddick was too busy attempting to change the world to spend time on such efforts, which she considered trivial. "In the business of skin and hair care, we

The headquarters of Anita Roddick's worldwide business, The Body Shop. By the mid-1980s, the company had become one of England's most successful international businesses and had made a fortune for its founders, Anita and Gordon Roddick.

don't advertise, but we garner an enormous amount of attention on some of our actions, whether liked or not liked," she said. "We're not an anonymous company because we stand for something—and we are claiming a territory where the competition won't follow."[11]

Roddick enjoyed the attention that her actions attracted. As her business grew, so did her desire to stand apart from other businesses around the world. Some people, however, questioned her motives. After all, she was making money off of people who had concerns about the way they looked. Even Roddick admitted on occasion that there was little evidence that all the lotions and creams in the world would keep people from aging. Yet at The Body Shop she spun the stories that sold her products.

Whether all of her tales were true or not no one seemed to know. "Being brought up with fables and fairy tales herself Anita Roddick believes in the power of stories," said one researcher who studied Roddick's business style. "Storytelling has become one of her leadership principles, which she has passionately practiced since the start of The Body Shop to motivate sales staff, but also to communicate."[12]

As a business leader, Roddick found that the information that she shared with her employees, her customers, and others helped them understand her passion for human rights. As The Body Shop continued to grow, more of her tales followed. "Whenever change comes up, I have to go back and tell the story," she said. "Those are the great anecdotes . . . it's the gatherer, the planter, the harvester, how do you make that become a story?"[13] Despite what some critics would later suggest, Roddick seemed to be honest in her appeal to customers interested in buying her products. "Our products won't make you ten years younger or irresistible to the opposite sex," a Body Shop fact sheet once said. "What they will do is cleanse, polish and moisturise."[14]

Roddick continued telling stories as The Body Shop expanded stores into other countries. Still, instead of buying advertisements, she used fact sheets and brochures, distributed directly to customers at her stores, as a way to spread the news. One brochure claimed that tea tree oil was "a little treasure from Down Under. A proven natural antibacterial cleanser—it has been used by Aborigines for over 40,000 years."[15] It was the early 1990s, and a dozen products were being created for The Body Shop in Australia for stores around the world.

It was in this way that Roddick continued to build The Body Shop fable. As more products were added to The Body Shop's line, more stories were told to accompany them. At times, Roddick went as far as saying that The Body Shop combined modern technology with ancient and traditional ideas.

DISLIKING COSMETICS COMPANIES

Still, Roddick's personal compassion for the world seemed to grow as her business grew. She advocated for fair trade, environmental protection, and social responsibility. And the more she learned about traditional cosmetics conglomerates, the less she liked these companies. Roddick never hid her true feelings. In fact, the bigger her business grew, the more outspoken she became. "Their marketing techniques were blatantly immoral," she wrote.[16] She also accused them of focusing on women's worst fears about aging. "I hate the beauty business," Roddick said. "It is a monster industry selling unattainable dreams. It lies. It cheats. It exploits women. Its major product lines are packaging and garbage."[17]

As The Body Shop continued to grow, Roddick and others in the company attended storytelling conferences to learn how to become more proficient at the craft. Managers were instructed to collect stories about employees' and customers' best and worst memories. The Body Shop retold those stories and polished them along the way. "We had storytelling as a form of management," she said. "It humanized the process so managing had to be part of gathering a story."[18]

Anita Roddick cared little if her business was built on a very untraditional model, because her ability to change the world was growing along with it. And that had long been one of her dreams.

The Body Shop Goes Public

It was 1981, just five years after Roddick has opened the first The Body Shop store, when she and Gordon started talking about going public. That meant that they would ask other people to purchase shares of stock in The Body Shop's company so that they would have more money to help their business grow. In that short time, The Body Shop had become an international company, with stores open in several other countries. Roddick could hardly believe how fast the company had grown, yet she and Gordon found themselves intrigued with building an even bigger business. "We were both enamored with the notion of seeing how far we could push The Body Shop idea," she said.[1]

The couple discussed the idea for a few years and, in 1984, decided the time was right. While Anita was still overseeing product development, store design, and public relations, Gordon was busy with financial and legal issues. With the help of an accounting firm and an attorney, the Roddicks were ready. They would invite other people to invest in their business.

The night before The Body Shop was to go to the London Stock Exchange, the Roddicks stayed overnight in London. They arrived at the Stock Exchange early the next morning, in time to see their company start getting investors when the exchange opened that morning. It was all very exciting. The entire event was a big deal to other people, too. The Body Shop had grown into one of England's most successful businesses, and the British Broadcasting Corporation (BBC) was even filming the stock sale.

By the time the sale was done, The Body Shop was worth $11 million. Anita and Gordon, personally, made about $2 million that day.[2] In a single day they saw their company become very valuable because other people were interested in investing in it and in seeing it grow. "We were now major shareholders in a public company which looked as if it was going to grow and grow," Anita said.[3]

Even though she was now very wealthy, nothing else changed about her life over the next few months. She still looked and dressed like a hippie. Having a lot of money meant that Roddick could put more focus on her concerns about the world. When they got back to Littlehampton the evening after the sale, she and Gordon sat in front of their fireplace and started talking about their future. They now had a lot more money to spend, but they certainly had no plans to retire or to go on a spending spree. Instead, they agreed their money would be used to help the world become a better place, while they continued to oversee The Body Shop's growth.

Roddick added an environmental projects department at The Body Shop's corporate headquarters to oversee the company's internal compliance with environmental issues. Environmental and energy-efficient details had been added to the building that housed the corporate headquarters. The company started buying bicycles to offer to their employees at a discount, hoping that employees would ride them to work to save gasoline. In addition, the company purchased energy-efficient trucks to make deliveries. "We don't breathe. We don't move unless we talk to them,"

A PRIVATE VS. A PUBLIC COMPANY

What is the difference between a private and a public company? Private companies are usually owned by one or more people, and the company's owners do not share details about their business with anyone. Public companies are owned by many people who buy shares in them and required by law to release information about their earnings and how much money their leaders make.

The Body Shop went from being a private company to becoming a public company when it was listed on the London Stock Exchange in April 1984. When The Body Shop shares were sold on the London Stock Exchange, Roddick became a millionaire because so many people decided to invest in her company.

A stock exchange is a collection of companies in which people can buy stock. A share of stock is the cost of owning a piece of a company. If you purchase stocks in a public company, then you can vote on issues involved in running that company and attend the company's annual investors' meeting. In other words, you get to voice an opinion about how that company is run.

Roddick said, regarding The Body Shop's environmental projects department.[4]

By now, The Body Shop was a big business. It had 250 shops on four continents. In 1985, Roddick received the Business Woman of the Year award in Britain; two years later, The Body Shop was named Company of the Year. She sent shareholders a company profile that featured a tree and the phrase, "Harm me not."[5] Roddick was certain that she would use this opportunity to continue building a strong company that had a very different focus.

People put money into the stock market so that they can make money with their shares. For example, if you buy a share of stock, it might cost you $20. But two years from now you may be able to sell that share for $35, so you would earn a profit of $15 from the sale of the stock. Some people make a lot of money by buying and selling stock shares.

Usually the owners of private companies decide they want more money to build their company, so they list on a stock exchange. If the company is in the United States, it might list on the New York Stock Exchange (NYSE) or NASDAQ. In Britain, a company usually lists on one of the oldest and largest stock exchanges in the world called the London Stock Exchange, also known as the LSE. Many companies outside of Britain also list on the LSE.*

---

* "The Role of the Exchange," The London Stock Exchange, http://www.londonstockexchange.com.

Anita Roddick, founder and managing director of The Body Shop, is seen in one of her London shops in September 1988. The enormous success of her business allowed her to concentrate more fully on environmental and social issues.

STILL TRAVELING

She continued to travel the world. In Japan, for example, she stumbled across a factory housing 7,000 nightingales, whose excrement was ground up and used as a cleanser to remove stains from silk, but she also learned that the excrement could also bleach the skin. That was one product that Roddick decided to avoid. Perhaps she thought it would be too hard to market. Instead, she talked to Japanese pearl divers about their body-care regimens, gaining tips that she hoped her company could eventually use.

Changing the world and helping the less fortunate was still Roddick's top priority. In 1987, with help from the International Boys Towns, she established an orphanage in

India, after she had contracted the group to make wooden massage rollers that would be sold in The Body Shop stores. She also regularly traveled to Nepal and Brazil, searching for natural oils, muds, and other products and practices that she could use in her business. During a 1989 trip to Nepal, she watched peasants make paper out of banana fibers and decided that, perhaps, The Body Shop could use more paper made in this way and thus dispense with the company's use of so much plastic.

Roddick also sought advice and input from other business owners who had ideas similar to her own. She was friends with the founders of Ben & Jerry's Ice Cream, a company that used an association called Cultural Survival to purchase rain forest nuts for its Rainforest Crunch ice cream. Cultural Survival is a nonprofit agency in the United States that focuses on helping tribal people throughout the world find ways that their customs can be used by others. The Body Shop soon partnered with Cultural Survival to find new products such as organic, natural nontimber seeds, nuts, resins, fruits, and essences from the rain forest. Cultural Survival earned some money from the partnership and used the proceeds to continue its tribal work.

Meanwhile, experts at Cultural Survival hailed The Body Shop as a company focused on the right things. "What The Body Shop does in terms of contribution of money and staff time to causes that they believe in—by way of environmental concerns or animal testing—no other corporation does," said one of its researchers.[6] "I think Anita's genius is identifying issues before other people do and getting the company to address them."[7]

One of Roddick's first campaigns after the company went public was with Greenpeace, an international environmental group that had never before partnered with a corporation. The Body Shop paid for a hundred posters to lobby against dumping hazardous waste in the North Sea.

Activists were invited to become Greenpeace members at their nearest The Body Shop store.

Roddick's next campaign was Save the Whales, which was also done in partnership with Greenpeace. Some of The Body Shop stores displayed posters and collection boxes for donations, and employees viewed an informative video about whaling. It was only after the high-profile Save the Whales campaign that some shareholders in The Body Shop started to worry that the company might be getting too political.

Interestingly, Roddick began finding it difficult to partner with Greenpeace groups all over the world because so many permissions were required, she later wrote in *Body and Soul*. Instead, she started working with a group called Friends of the Earth. It was through this partnership that The Body Shop did other earth-friendly campaigns.

CHALLENGES IN THE UNITED STATES

Through all of this, Roddick still did not have shops in the United States. She was worried about issues unique to America that she had not yet faced in other countries, such as labor unions that demanded fair wages, government regulations regarding goods that were imported, and the way many people in the United States shopped in malls instead of in downtown areas.

After receiving more than 2,500 requests from U.S. citizens who wanted to be franchisees, Roddick decided to move forward but decided she would take a new approach. [8] She hired a manager for the entire country, and stores in the United States began to open slowly, just one at a time.[9]

There was also more competition in the United States. The cosmetic company Estée Lauder had opened an environmentally conscious division called Origins, and The

GREENPEACE

Greenpeace is one of the largest and best-known nonprofit organizations formed to protect the environment. It has 250,000 members in the United States and 2.8 million members around the world. Founded in 1971, Greenpeace focuses on peaceful demonstrations against environmental ills. Its first protest was organized in 1971 when a group of citizens sailed in a fishing boat from Vancouver, British Columbia, to protest the United States' testing of nuclear missiles off a small Alaskan island known as Amchitka. Even though the boat and its protestors were intercepted by the U.S. Coast Guard, the protest attracted enough notice so that later that year nuclear testing ended on Amchitka, which became a bird refuge.

Some of Greenpeace's campaigns involve protesting against companies that produce waste that contributes to global warming, protecting the oceans and the forests, protesting nuclear power, exposing toxins in the environment, and other such endeavors. During one protest in 2009, campaigners unveiled a huge banner in the midst of a cleared section of the Indonesian rain forest. Just as President Barack Obama was preparing to attend the UN's climate summit, the banner declared, "Obama: you can stop this." Another group of protestors chained themselves to deforestation equipment in an attempt to stop the forest from being cleared.

Greenpeace is often known for its extreme protests that get its members into the news media so that they get more attention from the persons who make decisions on environmental issues. It has offices in 41 countries, and the Greenpeace headquarters is based in Amsterdam, in the Netherlands.

Limited, a clothing company, was about to open a line of stores called Bath & Body Works. By 1990, that company had already opened 100 stores across the United States.[10] Additionally, smaller boutiques were starting to open both in the United States and in Britain, nearly copying Roddick's business concept. Yet, confident about her success to date, she moved forward with opening stores in America.

Roddick was not happy about the competition she faced, as her shops opened slowly and her main competitor, Bath & Body Works, seemed to be opening in every mall around. In fact, she was haughty with a *Forbes* writer who tried to interview her about the situation. "Our business is about two things: social change and action, and skin care," she said. "Social change and action come first. You money-conscious people at *Forbes* just don't understand."[11] After years of trying a lot of different concepts, all of The Body Shop stores that opened followed the same prototype. The interiors were mainly green, and products were well organized along shelves on the walls and on stands in the middle of the floor. In keeping with her original defiance of fancy packaging, Roddick still saw to it that The Body Shop products were plainly packaged. An overwhelming aroma filled each store, drawing in customers from the outside. Shops were bright and had a sense of whimsy about them. This prototype, it seemed, worked well for the big business that she had created.

Roddick was good at telling The Body Shop's stories and advancing its mission. Note cards were lined up on shelves, each one explaining a specific product and why it was good for customers. She also began adding brochures in the shop that explained the business's stance against animal testing and other crusades. An encyclopedic book called *The Product Information Manual* was placed in each store so that customers could find out the ingredients of every product.

Eventually, stores were equipped with televisions showing videos either about the company's operational headquarters or about one of the causes it supported.[12]

Roddick's style of designing her stores grew out of her early years as a schoolteacher. She had discovered that her students responded very well to the bright graphics that she used in her classroom and to the soothing music that she sometimes played in the background. She designed her stores with a similar mind-set, believing these were places where people came to learn about products and causes around the world. The fact that products were being sold almost seemed incidental.

With corporate offices now in London, Roddick took the London Underground, also known as the tube, to work every day because it was most convenient for her. She usually wore jeans, sometimes a jacket, and very little jewelry. At the office, she encouraged employees to decorate windows to reflect the social causes they celebrated. Once, employees created a scene that looked like a harvest festival to emphasize the environmental problems caused by acid rain. At home, she planted a garden so that she would have a quiet place where she could spend time after work. Beyond indulging in her garden, she spent little on herself, rarely getting manicures or massages.

MAKING A DIFFERENCE, BEING A SUCCESS

Roddick wanted to live each day to its fullest, doing what she could to help humanity. "I mean, this is no dress rehearsal is it?" she once asked a reporter, admitting that she feared dying before she had made a contribution to the world.[13] She had little reason to fear: Authors and experts were already considering The Body Shop among the leaders of companies that had a new social and environmental consciousness. Her marketing strategy was praised as being forward thinking. "It cuts through the cynicism of consumers," wrote one analyst. "It clearly differentiates the company from its major competitors. . . . Customers feel that they are buying from a company whose values and business practices they know."[14]

The company became more sophisticated as it grew. Employees now underwent formal training at the London headquarters. Sales personnel were taught about the natural products, their origins, and how they should be used. The courses offered were so popular that the company had trouble training people as fast as they requested it. The Body Shop's employee newsletter focused far more on social causes than it did on sales training.

By 1990, The Body Shop had 320 stores in 37 countries, including 22 in the United States and more than 170 in Britain. At least 1,700 people worked for the company. Employees were given half days off to do community service work. It seemed that Roddick's management philosophy helped to build her company—the happier the employees, the more products they seemed to sell.

Stores continued emphasizing environmental concerns. Customers were given recycled bags for their purchases. Even the company's delivery trucks were considered to be vehicles on which Roddick could educate people about world causes. Sometimes trucks would be painted with scenes imploring protection of the rain forest; other times they would boast displays that encouraged education or concerns for human rights.[15] One slogan exclaimed, "If you think education is expensive, try ignorance." In Britain, The Body Shop even started its own conservation clubs, encouraging members to plant trees and to clean up beaches.[16]

By 1990, Roddick was hailed as a great leader. She was also extremely busy. She was invited to speak to cosmetic industry officials from around the world at the UN in New

In this 1986 photo, Anita Roddick gives a demonstration for Diana, Princess of Wales, at the opening of a new headquarters in Littlehampton, Sussex, England.

York City. In the United States, she launched a catalog business that employed disabled people to take calls. She took 35 top staff members to Romania for three weeks to work in neglected orphanages, part of a collaboration effort with a nonprofit organization based in Switzerland.[17] She received accolades from Britain's Princess Diana, and she contemplated opening shops in Russia.[18]

Roddick was confident. She thought she knew how to build a successful company. Going public had now provided the money she needed to fund that social consciousness. "It's the power of money, and if you can apply that money to good, so much the bloody better," she told a newspaper reporter.[19]

STILL A RENEGADE

As Roddick's business grew and her schedule became very demanding, she did not lose her personal focus. It was a cold night in January 1990 when she joined other environmentalists in a protest in front of the Brazilian embassy in London. Protestors had gathered to draw attention to an indigenous tribe in Brazil, the Yanomami Indians, who were being wiped out by diseases brought to their region by people who were searching for gold.

Roddick was concerned about the Indians because they were an important part of the rain forest, from which The Body Shop obtained some of its ingredients. The company organized an international campaign to draw attention to this cause. Stores around the world featured window displays, posters, T-shirts, brochures, and videotapes in an effort to educate customers about the Yanomami tribe. Before this nighttime protest, Roddick had allowed 250 of her employees to protest at the embassy in the daylight. Television crews had recorded the action.[20] No one, however, seemed surprised to see this millionaire businesswoman involved in a protest movement on the streets of London, since people around Britain were used to Roddick's renegade ways.

Despite what some people thought, Roddick did not get involved in just any cause. She chose causes that instilled passion in her customers and in her employees. She inspired young people to feel that they could change the world, no matter what cause The Body Shop was involved with. Roddick was a smart woman. She knew that if she inspired passion, then people would be passionate about buying The Body Shop products. The end result, she had already seen, was that the company would continue to grow bigger.

Roddick was very content in her personal life. She had a family that loved her. And she loved her job, which enabled

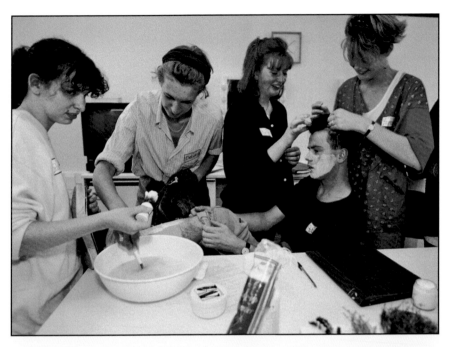

Staff members attend a class at The Body Shop Training School in London, England. Roddick believed her staff should be fully involved in all aspects of her business, as well as being passionately committed to her ideals.

her to be the person she had always wanted to be. Still, she would get annoyed when shareholders disagreed with her social concerns. She emphasized that the focus of the company was more about social change than high profits. Shareholders, though, invested in the company as a way to make more money. There seemed to be ongoing tension and some conflict. "My only duty is to my company and to keep it alive in a way I think is right and honest," she said. "I care more about the investment in spirit than the bloody investment in time and money."[21]

Some financial experts, however, cautioned that The Body Shop had not yet been through any hard times. Other business analysts suggested that for The Body Shop to grow, it would need to change its management structure. The company needed to start focusing more on its bottom line, they said. Although The Body Shop had grown by leaps and bounds, Roddick had little knowledge of the challenges that lay ahead.

Being Green

Anita Roddick was worried. During the 1990s, her company was growing so fast that she was afraid that the business would change. She felt like there were too many meetings and not enough fun. She told Gordon that they needed a department of surprises. She struggled to determine how to continue growing the already-large business. "Whatever we do we have to preserve that sense of being different," she said. "Otherwise, the time will come when everyone who works for us will say The Body Shop is just like every other company. It's big. It's monolithic. It's difficult . . . We just have to make sure we don't wind up like an ordinary company."[1]

Roddick's newest challenge was to keep her big company growing while balancing her personal life. She still spent a lot of her time working and traveling. Both of her daughters were now living on their own. Anita's mother, Gilda, was old and ailing and did not expect to live much longer. Roddick still held her mother in high esteem but was planning ahead for her death. "I think she is wonderful," she said. "She has such a right attitude for dealing with her coming death. At her funeral she wants everyone to dress in red, to play cha-cha-cha music."[2]

Roddick was also worried about herself. Now, nearly 50 years old, she felt like she had lost some of her feminine edge, which had enabled her to be a good businesswoman. Even though *Vogue* had crowned her the queen of cosmetics, Roddick was concerned because she knew it took a lot of spunk to be a good leader. "Once you're in a leadership role, your femininity is taken away because most leaders are men," she complained.[3]

Still, Roddick was considered an extremely successful business leader, and she had made progress on social issues as well. In 1989, The Body Shop Foundation had been launched to help focus a portion of Roddick's money on her three chief concerns: human rights, animal protection, and environmental protection. It was through the foundation that Roddick could focus on the issues about which she felt most passionate.

Roddick had changed little throughout the years. Despite being a very wealthy and popular business leader, she was still a conservationist. She rarely bought new clothes. She ran around her offices turning off lights that were not needed. To Roddick, an evening out meant inviting friends to her house for pizza.

By 1991, The Body Shop boasted 600 stores across the world. Roddick hoped that the number would grow to 1,000 by the year 2000. In no way was she or her company about to slow down. She continued planning for her future.[4]

Experts who studied her concept said she had a very simplistic view of how a business was run, because she believed that business was fairly simple and included only the buyer, the seller, and the environment in which transactions were done. "It's just buying and selling, with an added bit for me," she said. "It's trading. It's making your product so glorious that people don't mind buying it from you at a profit."[5]

Roddick still liked to travel to far-off places to make trades with local tribes. She visited the Wodaabe tribe in Africa and, after returning, burst into a meeting at her corporate headquarters with a sack full of potential Body Shop products. She met with the environmental minister of India at a London hotel, and the two women shared their ideas about moral values and leadership.[6] The bigger The Body Shop grew, it seemed, the more attention Roddick got. Her success now enabled her to meet and talk about business with a lot of important people around the world.

THE PRESSURES OF BUSINESS

With all of The Body Shop's growth, however, there were pressures. Shareholders pushed to make the company more profitable. Franchisees wanted to expand the number of stores they owned, and employees had their own expectations regarding company growth and what happened inside each store. What had once been entirely under Roddick's control, it seemed, now was everyone's business.

She found herself continually explaining the Quaker way of doing business, of caring about the customers, the employees, and society. This was Roddick's model for business, and she was sure it was the right one. "It's creating a new business paradigm," she explained. "It's showing that business can have a human face, and God help us if we don't try. It's showing that empowering employees is the key to keeping them, and that you empower them by creating a better educational system."[7]

Since Roddick's business had entered the U.S. marketplace, her involvement in social causes expanded to American interests. Although she was not a U.S. citizen, she used her stores as a place where voters could register and ended up signing up 50,000. She opposed the Persian Gulf War of 1990–1991, partnering with Amnesty International in her dissent. She started a Have a Heart campaign in the United States, and she encouraged customers to write to their representatives in Congress to oppose the U.S. intervention in the Persian Gulf. [8]

Meanwhile, The Body Shop stores flourished in America; by 1993, 120 stores had opened. Roddick continued her busy work with social causes and even formed an organization called Businesses for Social Responsibility with others, such as Ben & Jerry's Ice Cream and the shoe company Stride Rite. But the success of The Body Shop and its founder's steadfast focus on controversial social issues invited skepticism. Editors and writers often critiqued Roddick and her business. "She's doing an amazing thing by having environmental awareness and by doing some of her pro bonos, like offering people incentives for not driving to work," said author Debra Lynn Dadd. "However, I would say that from my standpoint, her products don't go far enough in terms of being environmentally safe."[9]

Although Dadd praised the company for some of its environmental practices, such as the use of recycled bags, she also criticized The Body Shop for using artificial colors, synthetic preservatives, and some ingredients that were not natural. Before long, others began voicing concerns as well. "They represent causes attractive to the liberal conscience. Yet this goodness is used, remorselessly, to sell vanity products," wrote an editor at *The Independent* in London. "You wash your hair in global concern."[10]

A BARRAGE OF CRITICISM

Meanwhile, franchisees in several countries revolted by saying that they could not make money in light of the strong competition from Bath & Body Works and other competitors.[11] In the mid-1990s, Roddick's admirers around the world were stunned by several reports filed by Jon Entine, a U.S. journalist who first wrote about her for the American magazine *Business Ethics*, and later in other publications. Entine had spent many hours traveling with Roddick. "These are the best times for Anita—everyone calls her by her first name. She is an international legend, part Robin Hood and part Mother Teresa," Entine wrote.[12]

He also joined Roddick on a visit to the Nanhu Indians of Mexico, where women were making exfoliating mitts sold by The Body Shop. The women were receiving only a cent for each mitt that they made. During her time there, Roddick pledged to give the villagers nearly anything they requested. "One village wanted a truck. Another asked for a tractor," said a young woman who had been hired by Roddick to work for her during the trip.

It was after this trip and several other jaunts that Entine questioned Roddick's motives in the articles that he wrote. He also alleged that she had stolen the idea for The Body Shop from the stores in Berkeley, California that she had visited as a young woman, that some of her products were not properly tested for bacteria, that some contaminated products were sold in The Body Shop stores, and that The Body Shop's ethics were bad. Entine claimed that the traditional media refused to question The Body Shop's practices, wanting to believe that Roddick was running a business that was focused on good environmental practices. Entine later quoted a corporate analyst who further critiqued Gordon and Anita Roddick's business practices. "The Roddicks are just not suited to be running a public company," said the analyst. "At the end of the day, [The] Body Shop is tired and dysfunctional."[13]

These reports stung Roddick. While eating roast beef sandwiches at her home with a reporter for the London *Daily Mail*, she attempted to counteract the bad publicity she was getting. She discussed the business she had built and the fact that she was 52 years old and personally facing the challenges of aging. In true Anita Roddick style, she was completely open with the male reporter. She confessed that her skin always felt dry, like parchment at times, and that she moisturized with mango butter. She talked about a potential new business strategy for The Body Shop, developing products for women who were aging.[14]

"Maybe the company would be more successful without me," said Roddick, acknowledging that her relentless campaigning for various causes might have been affecting the company's reputation. "If you stand up for things that people are uncomfortable with, especially if you're a woman, then you'll always be in for it."[15]

During the interview, Roddick also talked about visiting the natives of Brazil. "They probably think I'm a complete buffoon," she said. "I usually arrive with lots of music. I come with my Sony Walkman with two speakers."[16]

Roddick was in an introspective period. She had built a successful company that featured interesting stories about most of its products, but she knew that there were now critics watching her every move. While she inspired loyalty among many of her employees and customers who valued what she was doing, others were just as adamant that the business she had built was all a sham. One reporter noted:

Anita Roddick is seen here at a protest against animal testing for cosmetics. Her work in this area was instrumental in leading to a ban on such testing in Great Britain in 1998.

The shops exude a goody-goody feeling that makes you believe that you are caring about the planet and saving laboratory animals, even while buying some staggeringly superfluous bit of consumer nonsense like a peppermint foot lotion or elderflower eye gel.[17]

Roddick herself shrugged off such criticism. "If you take the moral high ground, you are bound to have critics," she said. "When we've made mistakes we've put procedures in place to prevent them from happening again.[18]

STOCKS TUMBLE

In the 1990s, as The Body Shop's stock prices started falling, the Roddicks took a close look at how their business was run. They even considered, briefly, making it a private company again and buying out their major shareholders. Instead, they decided to hire a new managing director who would work directly with Gordon and Anita to keep the company growing. For the first time in more than 20 years, Anita and Gordon were no longer the people at the head of their company, although they still made many of the major decisions. For example, the Roddicks planned to open stores in India, China, and South Africa.[19]

But other problems popped up, too. Roddick's good friend and one of her first employees, Aidre, involved The Body Shop in a lawsuit. Aidre owed money to a bank and blamed The Body Shop for not helping her meet financial targets for her fourth franchised store in England.[20]

Despite the financial concerns, Roddick continued to focus on social issues. In 1998, The Body Shop collected 4 million signatures on petitions that eventually led to a ban on animal testing for the cosmetics industry in Britain.[21] She also started a women's awareness campaign through the 1,500 stores that now existed around the world. The Body Shop released a doll called Ruby, a plump, Barbie-like toy, to emphasize that women come in all shapes and sizes. With the doll's release, the company kicked off a campaign called "Love your body." It followed with other themes focused on self-esteem, activism, and aging.[22]

Meanwhile, on the London Stock Exchange, The Body Shop hit a three-year low. That meant that big changes were in store for Roddick and her company. "I've never really understood what my role was," she said. "I've done marketing, style, image, shop design and public relations."[23] Although she served as cochair with Gordon, Roddick's focus was really more on social causes than on the company itself. Her reputation regarding social rights was strong, and nonprofit groups started asking her to be more involved in their operations. She was a director of

Seattle police use tear gas to push back World Trade Organization pro-testers in downtown Seattle, Washington, on November 30, 1999. The protests delayed the opening of the WTO third ministerial conference. Anita Roddick was among the protesters who were gassed.

Human Rights Watch, based in New York City, and of a group called Unrepresented People and Nations, based in Holland. She helped fund a week of educational seminars on economic corporate globalization and then took part in a huge protest during which she was tear-gassed at the World Trade Organization in Seattle, Washington, in 1999. All of this enhanced her image as a business leader who believed that global concerns should come before corporate profits.

Roddick traveled the world to share her ideas about human rights, wrote newspaper columns about her favorite causes, and lobbied government officials.[24] She was still, however, interested in what her stores were doing. Even though she had a global perspective, she impacted small communities, too. In the New York City neighborhood of Harlem, for example, The Body Shop donated five percent of the store's sales receipts to the Harlem Community Giving Program.

By August 2000, however, Roddick was seriously questioning her position within her now huge company. Its competitors were battering her business in some countries, and critics continued to claim that her green consciousness

HUMAN RIGHTS WATCH

Human Rights Watch is a nonprofit organization that focuses on protecting people around the world. Among the human rights abuses that the organization brings to light are ones right here in the United States: children, for example, who are forced to work in farm fields and are sometimes exposed to toxic pesticides.

The organization addresses different issues in other countries, too. The group also works to rid the world of land mines left behind from wars, protests against the abuse of women's rights in Afghanistan, and protests against the abuse of detainees in China. The organization also pays close attention to the infringement of the rights of women, especially in third-world countries; minorities; homosexuals; and other disenfranchised groups.

With financial help from private donations and foundations, the organization works with various groups and enterprises. It also works directly with governments in many countries to help design and endorse laws that will protect children and adults who face problematic circumstances. For more information on this organization, visit http://www.humanrightswatch.com.

The Dalai Lama *(center)* salutes the crowd, accompanied by the Amnesty International France president, Pierre Sane, and Anita Roddick, at the Amnesty International concert given in Paris, France, on December 10, 1998, to celebrate the fiftieth anniversary of the signing of the Universal Declaration of Human Rights.

was not authentic. She and Gordon began thinking about selling the business they had nurtured and loved.[25] As usual, they discussed their next business move for several months. Just as they had when they owned the restaurant years ago, they were careful to think through all of their options. Was now the right time to sell? Should they continue to stay involved, but not quite as much?

Still, Roddick was hailed as a great business leader and, despite the criticism, many people still recognized her as an environmental activist. In Washington, D.C., she accepted the Entrepreneurial Champion Award from a group of 200 women who met regularly to support each other's endeavors. During the same trip, she visited the

Washington headquarters of consumer advocate and activist Ralph Nader. She also posed on a bridge for the cover of *Ms* magazine.[26]

The trip to Washington summed up Anita Roddick's place at this period in her life. Despite all of the criticism and her doubts about her role in The Body Shop, she was still known throughout the world for her environmentally sensitive business practices. Only time would tell whether she and Gordon would move forward with plans to sell their shares in the business they had built.

Big Changes

Although Roddick had become known as the queen of green, her critics sometimes called her the Mother Teresa of capitalism. The interesting products and amazing stories from The Body Shop had developed loyal customers in the United States, Britain, and many other countries. Even though Roddick's environmental principles had been questioned and critiqued, her business was still raging in many parts of the world.

Competition had been tough, especially in the United States, where Bath & Body Works had taken a strong lead, featuring similar products but without a socially conscious marketing plan. The Body Shop was still making money, but not nearly as much as it had made during its first 15 years in business. By 2001, there were 1,800 stores worldwide.

Roddick talked about reinventing her business. She started looking at selling health foods in the company's stores. The Body Shop also started hosting parties in people's homes in the United States, allowing independent representatives to sell its lotions and soaps. Yet at the same time, Roddick had become one of the biggest critics of her own company. No longer did she seem to care what anyone said or wrote about her. She announced one day that 80 percent of The Body Shop's products were useless. She admittedly disliked a new line of Juice It gel products that were created by others within the company and were selling well.[1] The company continued to try new products, but some flopped, including those that featured strange ingredients such as Tobacco Flower cosmetics and Palm Shine shampoo.[2]

The Roddicks and others involved in their business started talking about selling the stores in the United States, where Anita said she did not understand the culture of customers. One of her concerns was that many mall managers were against the fact that The Body Shop stores campaigned for causes. At one time, the U.S. Drug Enforcement Agency even examined hemp products sold in The Body Shop stores because they contained traces of THC—the main psychoactive substance in cannabis. But the idea to sell only the U.S. division did not work out. Meanwhile, Gordon and Anita continued talking about selling the entire business.

There was another concern in Anita Roddick's life. She was devastated to learn that Gordon had had an extramarital affair. And, to make matters even worse, because it was public knowledge, everyone kept asking questions about it. Sometimes Anita avoided the questions, other times she called it a "near death" experience to learn of his unfaithfulness.[3] The Roddicks decided to work on their marriage and stayed together.

WRAPPING UP A CAREER

At the turn of the new century, Anita started hinting that she was ready to wrap up her career as a businesswoman. At this point, Anita and Gordon Roddick were very wealthy. (They controlled 51 percent of The Body Shop business with Ian McGlinn, the auto repairman who had loaned Anita money many years before. McGlinn still owned half of their shares.) "I'm not sure how much longer I'm going to hang around the company," she said. "After 25 years, I want the political freedom to do the things I want to do. I don't want to keep on emoting about the shape of a bottle or whether or not we should go for elderberry body butter. I love this company, but I need breathing space."[4]

Roddick also admitted that the older she grew, the blunter and more radical became her concerns for social causes. "It is a lie that anti-aging creams will get rid of wrinkles," she told British reporters one day. "Moisturisers do work, but the rest is complete pap."[5] Roddick's comments about both the business and social causes made news around the world. Business analysts agreed that her statements could hurt The Body Shop business even more. People within the company were never quite sure what they would hear when Anita was out traveling the world. She made headlines again when she went to the Edinburgh Book Festival in Scotland to sign copies of her new book, *Business as Unusual*. "The Body Shop is now a dysfunctional coffin," she said while there.[6]

As time wore on, both Anita and Gordon began talking with various companies about buying The Body Shop business. Anita continued to be frustrated while working with the board of directors that oversaw The Body Shop. They seemed to lose respect for her decisions, and unlike in the early years of The Body Shop being a public company, they were no longer afraid to disagree when she expressed rebel ideas. At one time she wanted to hang signs in The Body Shop stores that said "Shame on you Bush," regarding a decision made by President George H.W. Bush. The board refused to move forward with the campaign, fearing that it would hurt business.[7]

Still, she did not stop voicing her opinions. While being interviewed by newspaper and television reporters, she talked more about politics than business and very little about her two daughters, now in their late twenties and early thirties, and her three young grandchildren. (One daughter, Justine, had moved far away to California and was happy there. The other, Samantha, stayed in England to raise her children. Anita and Gordon bought a house in California, near Justine.)[8]

After 25 years of running her business, Roddick complained that fewer employees listened to her, too. Despite continually brainstorming new ideas, sometimes people looked at her as if she did not know what she was talking about. When she visited the Soapworks factory in Scotland, which created bars of soap sold at The Body Shop stores, she suggested that the factory produce bars of oud, a molasses-like substance taken from the trunks of the agarwood tree found in the Middle East. Then, as they always had, Roddick's suggestions just kept coming. Workers looked around at each other, perhaps wondering if she was sane, as she tried to inspire them to have a weekend Italian art party, featuring artists, music, and food, to get more local recognition. No one, it seemed, could believe that this very wealthy woman was imploring them to have some little weekend festival just for fun.[9]

She also continued to irk reporters. When Roddick later met with a writer for a Canadian magazine, their interview confirmed her reputation. "She motormouths her way through our more or less one-way conversation," complained the writer.[10]

At the same time, she launched campaigns to discourage corporate executives in countries such as the United Kingdom and the United States from setting up their own factories in third-world countries. "I want a financial bottom line that includes human rights and social justice," she said.[11] She also tried to get other companies and manufacturers to buy products from community trade organizations that marketed items from third-world countries. (Fair trade organizations protected the poor people in third-world countries by encouraging major corporations to pay fair prices for products.) Roddick was disappointed that, after the many years she had spent emphasizing such trade, few companies got involved. "I'm desperate to find another company to buy products from some of the community trade organizations we've set up," she said. "We're trying to get Avon involved. If the companies won't do it, we'll go to their suppliers and manufacturers."[12]

Roddick now sensed that, when it came to politics, no one wanted to listen to her. "The left wing doesn't like me because I make money," she complained. "The right wing hates me because I'm challenging financial institutions."[13] Academics, however, were another matter. Roddick's views were so unique, in fact, that academics around the world frequently invited her to talk to their students about her business practices and entrepreneurship. "Dysfunction is the essence of entrepreneurship," she wrote on her blog in 2001. "I've had dozens of requests from places like Harvard and Yale to talk about the subject. It makes me laugh that ivy leaguers are so keen to 'learn' how to be entrepreneurs, because I'm not convinced it's a subject you can teach. I mean, how do you teach obsession?"[14]

At the London School of Economics, a renowned college attended by future business leaders, she went on a tirade about corporations and their greediness. Ironically,

Roddick recognized that if she had not built a profitable company, no one would listen to her, including the media.

The tables turned a bit in 2002, when Roddick herself became the focus of a protest in the United States. After the first anniversary of the terrorist attacks of September 11, 2001, The Body Shop stores were boycotted because of remarks Roddick made about the infringement on free speech and other civil liberties in the aftermath of the attacks. [15] Even though Roddick was not alone in her concerns, the conservative *New York Post* called her the "Body Shop bubblehead" and the "self-righteous diva of cocoa butter." Despite such criticisms, Roddick rallied around the idea that social protest was the only way to effect change. "It's got to be a movement," she said. "A people-powered movement."[16]

When people questioned Roddick about why she continued to work so hard for social change, she was quick to answer. "If I don't do this stuff, it's like death to me," she said. "I managed by total accident . . . to trip over an idea of creating wealth and position and empowerment and resources for a lot of people. . . . I'm bloody going to use it for public good."[17]

CHANGES

In early 2002, Anita and Gordon made a major decision. They resigned as cochairs and stopped participating in the day-to-day operations of their company. Gordon said he would spend more time on The Body Shop Foundation. Anita was interested in attracting a wider audience for activism. Besides writing *Body and Soul*, she also published *Brave Hearts, Rebel Spirits*, a collection of short pieces about activism written by Brooke Shelby Biggs. She also edited another book titled *A Revolution of Kindness*, a collection of essays from other writers. She continued to travel around the world, lecturing when she had the opportunity.

In addition, she started thinking about creating a line of clothing for young activists.

"What we should be thinking about is enterprise and livelihood creation," she told entrepreneurs who gathered to hear her talk in Singapore.

> You get out of university now and there's no guarantee of a job. But what we should be training and encouraging people to do is to ask: What are your skills, what are your talents, and what are your interests? You mush them together to make a livelihood that gives you independence, freedom and enough money to make your needs well met.[18]

As Roddick now approached 60 years old, she was surprised when England's Queen Elizabeth II named her a dame, an honorary title similar to a knighthood given to men by the British monarch. Even though Roddick sometimes complained that no one was listening, it was apparent that even the Queen of England recognized her achievements.

Meanwhile, sales at The Body Shop improved for the first time in years. "The Body Shop has grown up," claimed its chief executive, Peter Saunders, who hoped to attract more affluent buyers by modernizing the stores. "Through the years, just like many women, we've experimented with quite a few stages. Now we are where we want to be with a good, high quality style." Through all of this, Saunders stressed that, although profits were important, so was the social responsibility that Roddick had instilled in the company. Still, it was apparent that The Body Shop was changing. It was being regenerated as something other than Roddick's initial company vision.[19]

Even though Anita and Gordon owned a large percentage of the company, there were more disagreements with

Dame Anita Roddick, founder of The Body Shop, stands with the dame commander medal she received from Queen Elizabeth II at Buckingham Palace in London, England, on November 13, 2003. Roddick was given the honor for her services to retailing, the environment, and charity.

the corporate managers. The media now reported that the Roddicks were serious about selling the company. "Where we have reached with The Body Shop is not really what

I would have wanted when I first started up," confessed Roddick to a reporter for the *Toronto Star*. "I think if I had known back then how it would all turn out, I would have slit my wrists."[20]

Roddick was uncomfortable with the large size of the company and how it was being run. Workers in the Soapworks plant in Scotland protested against her when they did not get the raises they wanted, even though she no longer made such day-to-day salary decisions.[21]

She and Gordon continued to talk to many potential buyers. Eventually, the Roddicks met with Sir Lindsay Owen-Jones, the chairman of the global cosmetics company known as L'Oréal. Anita liked Owen-Jones very much. "There is something quite different about L'Oréal, a sense of courteousness," Roddick said.[22]

It was not long before a deal would be made.

SELLING OUT

News that the Roddicks had sold their shares in the company started spreading like wildfire. Many of Anita's loyal fans and followers were angry. They accused her of selling out, just for the money. L'Oréal, they complained, still tested products on animals. "She appears to be taking the money and running," said the director of an organization called Naturewatch.[23] On June 9, 2006, L'Oréal officially purchased The Body Shop. "It was the last day of any ownership I had in that crazy complicated company I founded," she wrote on her blog, which she planned to use to chart her work on social causes. [24]

Indeed, The Body Shop had sold for $1.1 billion, much of which went to other shareholders, in addition to the Roddicks. Anita and Gordon would earn approximately $204 million from the sale, a figure that would be evenly split between the two of them. "I don't believe that L'Oréal will compromise the ethics of The Body Shop," Roddick told a reporter right after the sale. "That is after all what they are paying for and they are too intelligent to mess with our DNA."[25]

After all the stress of recent years, Roddick was happy to be rid of the company. She described it as the best thirtieth anniversary present The Body Shop could receive. "At my age, I am grateful for an approximate solution," she said.[26]

The sale was front-page news in London's most notable newspapers and was a popular topic on television. The day that the sale was officially announced, journalists peppered Roddick with questions as she went to meet L'Oréal's chairman at a London hotel. Instead of justifying the sale, Roddick talked about something different to distract the reporters. She started discussing door-to-door sales and how women who do this help other people from being lonely. She was hoping that her comments would draw attention away from the amount of money that she had just made and refocus reporters on social causes.

When the media conference was over, she hugged the L'Oréal executives and quickly left to visit a nearby Body Shop. Once in the store, Anita tried to get used to not being the owner anymore. She explained to employees and customers what had just happened with the sale. Later the same day, she called her 92-year-old mother, who still lived in Littlehampton and was planning her own funeral. (She had recently requested that Roddick cremate her body and put her ashes into fireworks that would be exploded in the sky.) Then, Anita and Gordon took their younger daughter, Samantha, and their grandchildren out for pizza.

The day of the sale did not end without Roddick engaging in a social cause. Her latest concern was to free prisoners in Louisiana who had helped organize a recovery effort after Hurricane Katrina hit New Orleans and the surrounding area. "The Black Panthers are great community organizers," she told a reporter.[27]

AFTER THE BODY SHOP

At first, Roddick was annoyed with the people who accused her of selling out. But within days, she got busy distributing her money and making sure she was immersed in as many social causes as possible. As Roddick had promised, more than $100 million of her personal wealth was funneled into her charity work through The Roddick Foundation.

It was only a few months later that she was confronted with a new challenge. Routine blood tests revealed that Roddick had Hepatitis C, an illness that she had received after getting a blood transfusion when she gave birth to Samantha, 30 years earlier. Because she had had the illness for so long without being diagnosed, the Hepatitis C had caused her to develop cirrhosis of the liver, a disease that could eventually kill her. "What I can say is that having hep C means that I live with a sharp sense of my own mortality—which in many ways makes life more vivid and immediate," she wrote on her blog. "It makes me even more determined to just get on with things."[29]

Certainly, getting on with things is what Roddick did best. Following her diagnosis, she began a campaign to get the United Kingdom to recognize Hepatitis C in more persons who carry it and to encourage people to be tested. Roddick became active in the Hepatitis C Trust, which had already been established in Britain a few years earlier. "In a way, campaigning with the Heptatitis C Trust is business as usual for me," she said. "Speaking out about my hep C is just carrying on what I helped to start at The Body Shop. Life has just taken a more interesting turn."[30]

Still, it seemed that Anita Roddick now had just one more cause to add to her list. Among other engagements, she met with the leader of a group called Reprieve, which provided legal and other support to people facing the death penalty, and she agreed to become the chair of Reprieve's board of directors for the following year. Instantly, she started making plans for Reprieve's staff members to spend time at a retreat in her home.

No one, however, was prepared for what happened next. Roddick was at home when she complained of a headache.

DID YOU KNOW?

Anita Roddick's spirit of creativity, entrepreneurialism, and courage are honored by The Roddick Foundation, which was established before Anita died but lives on today by providing grants to organizations that reflect her principles.

In *Business as Unusual*, Roddick proclaimed that she would die poor. Even though she had become very wealthy by the time her book came out in 2000, she planned to donate all of her money to charity after her death. An inundation of requests from various charities that wanted a piece of her wealth followed this proclamation.

These requests led Roddick to write a blog post a on her Web site on December 16, 2005, asking fans to leave her alone. She wrote:

> What I am going to do is set up a charitable foundation, through which donations will be made to groups and individuals that show leadership in the areas of global justice, human rights, environmental action and grassroots organising. But we won't be accepting unsolicited requests. . . . Please give me a break—I'm not dead yet!

After Roddick died of a brain tumor in 2007, charities all over the world began to benefit from her generosity. The Roddick Foundation is still a family-run, independent organization that gives away millions of dollars to organizations involved

After she collapsed, she was rushed to St. Richard's Hospital in Chichester, England, where she died of a brain tumor. It was September 10, 2007. Anita Roddick was only 64 years old. Gordon and her daughters were by her side.

It was Gordon who posted the next blog message. "At 6:30 p.m. on Monday, 10th September, someone reached

in human rights, as well as social, labor, and environmental justice. The organization's mission statement perfectly represents Anita Roddick after her death: "Our foundation is dedicated to those who change the world."

Among groups that have benefited from funding received through The Roddick Foundation are the United Kingdom's branch of Amnesty International; the Angola 3 Campaign, which was organized just prior to Roddick's death to release three activist prisoners from the Louisiana Penitentiary after they provided much help in the aftermath of Hurricane Katrina; the National Labor Committee, which provides funds to protect worker rights around the world; Reprieve, an organization that fights for the rights of those who are facing the death penalty; the Hepatitis C Trust, with which Roddick was very involved just prior to her death; Body & Soul, an organization that gives support to children, teens, and families living with HIV; Friends of the Earth, an environmental protection organization; the Rainforest Action Network; and many others.

You can read more about The Roddick Foundation at http://www.theroddickfoundation.org. For those interested in the causes supported by The Roddick Foundation, visit http://www.anitaroddick.com, where Anita Roddick's team continues to write blog entries and post news links about environmental, social, and human injustices around the world.

into my heart and turned out all of the lights," he wrote. "In an instant that funny, vibrant woman who was my life, lover and closest friend was gone."[31]

Gordon was devastated. The news struck everyone that one of Britain's greatest business minds was gone. Even Prime Minister Tony Blair made a statement. "She campaigned for green issues for many years before it became fashionable," he said, "and inspired millions to the cause by bringing sustainable products to a mass market."[32]

THE GREEN QUEEN LIVES ON

Just a few days after her death, a small private funeral was held. Roddick's body was placed in a biodegradable coffin, and she had instructed her family to be sure she was cremated in a "carbon-neutral" way. After a brief funeral service, mourners were served a buffet featuring locally grown lamb and vegan sandwiches.[33]

More than a month later, though, Roddick was honored at the Central Hall in London's Parliament Square, on what would have been her sixty-fifth birthday, in a service organized by Gordon and her daughters. Photos of Anita with her family, as well as photos of her working on her many social causes, were displayed in the lobby. Her favorite poem from Walt Whitman's *Leaves of Grass* was posted in large letters. Following a collage of some of the videos that Roddick had taped for The Body Shop years earlier, representatives of Roddick's many causes and organizations spoke in her memory. At the end, there was a standing ovation.

Outdoors, Roddick's image was beamed larger-than-life onto the side of London's National Theatre as thousands of people marched in the chilly autumn air carrying candles and placards that said "I am an Activist."[34] Later that evening, 500 biodegradable balloons were released into the night sky.

People hold banners as they walk across Westminster Bridge in London, England, as part of a procession in memory of Anita Roddick, who died on September 10, 2007.

"Dying is commonplace," said Gordon, "but a life well lived is rare."[35]

Since Roddick's death, writers and academics around the world have continued to study and praise her work. "Roddick's genius was to marry her gift for narrative to her passion for the environment and fair trade," wrote one professor the year following her death. "Body Shop was not about shampoo, it was about ethical consumerism, the fight against AIDS and putting pressure on governments to focus on poverty. We bought the foot lotion because we liked the idea behind it."[36]

Indeed, he was right.

Anita Roddick made it her business to expose consumers to the great needs of the world. The stories she wrote about her products helped reveal the existence of far-off lands to many people who never were able to travel there. With The Body Shop, Roddick proved that business could be done differently, that profits and activism were not mutually exclusive interests.

CHRONOLOGY

1942 Anita Lucia Perilli is born in Littlehampton, England.

1950 Gilda, Anita's mother, marries Henry, who is Anita's real father.

1963 Anita begins traveling the world.

1969 Anita gives birth to her first child, Justine.

1971 Anita, Gordon, and Justine travel to the United States; Samantha is born in July in England; Anita and Gordon buy St Winifred's hotel in Littlehampton.

1972 Anita and Gordon open Paddington's restaurant in Littlehampton.

1976 On March 26 Anita opens her first The Body Shop store in Brighton, England. A second store opens in Chichester after she borrows money from Ian McGlinn.

1977 Gordon returns from his horseback trip in South America to help Anita with The Body Shop.

1984 The Body Shop begins selling shares on the stock market, making millionaires of the Roddicks.

1985 The Body Shop partners with Greenpeace in a campaign to end toxic dumping in the North Sea.

1986 The Save the Whales campaign, a partnership between Greenpeace and The Body Shop, commences.

1988 The first The Body Shop store opens in New York City.

1989   Anita travels back to Nepal to visit the Nyinba tribe.

1994   The Body Shop sets up a Community Trade Program.

1995   The Roddicks consider buying back shares of The Body Shop to make it a private company again.

1996   The Body Shop comes under intense public scrutiny for some of its environmental practices.

1998   The Body Shop collects 4 million signatures on petitions, which eventually leads to a ban on animal testing for the cosmetics industry in Britain.

2002   The Roddicks step down as cochairs of The Body Shop.

2006   The Body Shop is sold to L'Oréal.

2007   Anita begins talking about having Hepatitus C; she dies on September 10 of a brain tumor.

NOTES

CHAPTER 1

1. Lynn Barber, "The Lynn Barber Interview: Fruitful Fidget," *The Independent* (London). March 3, 1991, p. 3.
2. Deborah Stead, "Managing: Secrets to a Cosmic Cosmetician," *New York Times*. September 23, 1990, Sec. 3, p. 25.
3. Barber, "Interview: Fruitful Fidget."
4. Miho Nagano, "She was a Cosmetic Crusader," *Investor's Business Daily*. April 9, 2008, p. A4.
5. Anita Roddick, *Body and Soul*. New York: Crown Publishers, 1991, p. 102.
6. Ibid., p. 73.
7. Ibid., p. 167.
8. Ibid., p. 168.
9. Deborah Stead, "Managing: Secrets to a Cosmic Cosmetician," *New York Times*. September 23, 1990, Sec. 3, p. 25.
10. Phillip Elmer-Dewitt and Elizabeth Lea, "Anita the Agitator," *Time*. January 25, 1993.
11. Russell Miller, "Did the Green Goddess Sell Out?" *Daily Mail*. September 12, 2007, p. 36.
12. Barber, "Interview: Fruitful Fidget."

CHAPTER 2

1. Roddick, *Body and Soul*, p. 29.
2. Ibid.
3. Ibid.
4. Barber, "Interview: Fruitful Fidget."
5. Susie MacKenzie, "Women: Prophet and Gloss— Public Lives—Anita Roddick," *Guardian* (London). September 11, 1991.
6. Roddick, *Body and Soul*, p. 37.
7. Barber, "Interview: Fruitful Fidget."

8. "Pioneering Body Shop Founder Who Fought for Green Issues," *Irish Times*. September 15, 2007.
9. "Anita Roddick—Business Thinkers and Management Giants," *Bloomsbury Business Library*. 2007, p. 37.
10. Roddick, *Body and Soul*, p. 48.
11. Ibid., p. 49.
12. Elmer-Dewitt and Lea, "Anita the Agitator."
13. Roddick, *Body and Soul*, p. 51.
14. Ibid., p. 53.

CHAPTER 3

1. Roddick, *Body and Soul*, p. 55.
2. Andrew Alderson, "Gordon Roddick: I Want to Do Anita Justice," *Sunday Telegraph*. October 21, 2007, p. 27.
3. Roddick, *Body and Soul*, p. 56.
4. Ibid., p. 56.
5. Alderson, "Gordon Roddick."
6. Lucy Johnson, "Husband's Vow to Keep the Flame of Dame Anita's Legacy Alive," *Sunday Express*. February 17, 2008, p. 38.
7. Anita Roddick, *Business as Unusual*. London: Anita Roddick Publications, 2005, p. 35.
8. Jon Entine, "Anita Roddick's Unfair Trade," *Mail on Sunday*. September 16, 2007.
9. Roddick, *Body and Soul*, p. 60.
10. Roddick, *Business as Unusual*, p. 35.
11. Roddick, *Body and Soul*, p. 61.
12. Ibid., p. 62.
13. Roddick, *Business as Unusual*, p. 36.
14. Ibid., p. 36.
15. Nicola M. Pless, "Understanding Responsible Leadership: Role Identity and Motivational Drivers," *Journal of Business Ethics*. 74: 437–56 (2007).

CHAPTER 4

1. Roddick, *Body and Soul*, p. 67.
2. MacKenzie, "Women: Prophet and Gloss."
3. Roddick, *Body and Soul*, p. 68.
4. Ibid., p. 73.
5. Ibid., p. 74.
6. Annette Boulter, "I Was Her First Shop Worker: She Was My Inspiration," *Times* (London). September 12, 2007.
7. Ibid.
8. Ibid.
9. Roddick, *Body and Soul*, p. 82.
10. Miller, "Green Goddess."
11. Roddick, *Body and Soul*, p. 86.
12. "Leader as Social Advocate: Building the Business by Building Community," *Leader to Leader*. Summer 2000, pp. 20–25.

CHAPTER 5

1. Roddick, *Body and Soul*, p. 70.
2. Ibid.
3. "Leader: Building Community."
4. Alice Miles, "Roddick's Ruse: It Wasn't the Moisteriser After All," *Times* (London). September 12, 2007, p. 19.
5. Roddick, *Body and Soul*, p. 97.
6. Pless, "Understanding Responsible Leadership."
7. "Leader as Social Advocate."
8. Miles, "Roddick's Ruse."
9. "Leader as Social Advocate."
10. Ibid.
11. Ibid.
12. Pless, "Understanding Responsible Leadership."
13. Ibid.

14. Tara Brabazon, "Buff Puffing an Empire: The Body Shop and Colonization by Other Means," *Journal of Media & Cultural Studies*. 15:2 (2001), pp. 187–200.

15. Ibid.

16. Roddick, *Body and Soul*, p. 96.

17. Ibid., p. 9.

18. Pless, "Understanding Responsible Leadership."

CHAPTER 6

1. Roddick, *Body and Soul*, p. 106.

2. Elmer-Dewitt and Lea, "Anita the Agitator."

3. Roddick, *Body and Soul*, p. 107.

4. Christina Robb, "Whole-earth Beauty: Body Shop's Founder Trots the Globe in Quest of Effective—and Environmentally Safe—Cosmetic Products," *Boston Globe*. September 15, 1990, p. 9.

5. Catherine Bennett, "Look: Power of the Body Politic," *Sunday Times* (London). March 6, 1988.

6. Robb, "Whole-earth Beauty."

7. Ibid.

8. Jean Sherman Chatzky, "Changing the World," *Forbes*. March 2, 1992, pp. 83–87.

9. Ibid.

10. Ibid.

11. Bo Burlingham, "The Woman Has Changed Business Forever," Mansueto Ventures. June 1990, p. 34.

12. Ibid.

13. Penny Vicenzi, "Labour and Love," *Times* (London). June 19, 1987.

14. Burlingham, "Woman Changed Business."

15. Deborah Stead, "Managing: Secrets."

16. Robb, "Whole-earth Beauty."

17. Ibid.

18. Bennett, " Body Politic."

19. Burlingham, "Woman Changed Business."
20. Ibid.
21. Bennett, "Body Politic."

CHAPTER 7

1. Burlingham, "Woman Changed Business."
2. MacKenzie, "Women: Prophet and Gloss."
3. Jessica Davies, "Why Women Can't Have Power and Sexuality," *Daily Mail* (London). February 12, 1993.
4. MacKenzie, "Women: Prophet and Gloss."
5. Burlingham, "Woman Changed Business. "
6. Barber, "Interview: Fruitful Fidget."
7. Burlingham, "Woman Changed Business."
8. Elmer-Dewitt and Lea, "Anita the Agitator."
9. Robb, "Whole-earth Beauty."
10. Brabazon, "Buff Puffing."
11. Entine, "Roddick's Unfair Trade."
12. Ibid.
13. Jon Entine, "A Social and Environmental Audit of The Body Shop: Anita Roddick and the Question of Character," July 1996. http://www.jonentine.com/the-body-shop.html.
14. Simon Garfield, "Anita and a Case of Fruit and Nuts . . . ," *Daily Mail* (London). October 10, 1994, p. 9.
15. Ibid.
16. Ibid.
17. Barber, "Interview: Fruitful Fidget."
18. Anne Simpson, "Mother Nature," *Courier Mail* (Brisbane, Australia). October 28, 2000, p. L7.
19. Rufus Olins, "Body Shop Goes for a New Shape," *Sunday Times* (London). June 1, 1997.

20. Patrick Tooher, "Roddick Falls Out with Oldest Friend," *The Independent* (London). October 1, 1995, p. 1.

21. Miho Nagano, "She Was a Cosmetic Crusader."

22. Stuart Elliot, "The Body Shop's Campaign Offers Reality, Not Miracles," *New York Times*. August 26, 1997.

23. Roger Cowe, "Body Blow," *Guardian* (London). May 13, 1998, p. 2.

24. Linda Yeung, "Anita Roddick Takes the Global Point of View," *South China Morning Post*. November 30, 1997, p. 2.

25. Entine, "Roddick's Unfair Trade."

26. Anita Roddick, "Diary, Anita Roddick," *New Statesman*. October 16, 2000.

CHAPTER 8

1. Simpson, "Mother Nature."

2. Dominic Rushe, "Body and Soul for Sale," *Sunday Times* (London). April 15, 2001, p. 5.

3. Ibid.

4. John Chapman, "Body Blow to Body Shop as Founder Anita Quits," *Sunday Express*. September 17, 2000.

5. Miranda Devine, "Wrinkle Queen Bursts the Bubble of Hope," *Daily Telegraph*. October 23, 2000, p. 23.

6. Matthew Beard, "Anita Roddick Says Body Shop Has Become a 'Dysfunctional Coffin,'" *The Independent* (London). August 25, 2001, p. 5.

7. Robert Crampton, "Out of Body Experience," *Times* (London). May 26, 2001, p. 38.

8. Ibid.

9. Ibid.

10. Susan G. Cole, "The True Colours of Anita Roddick," *Now Magazine* (Toronto), Spring 2001, p. 46.

11. Noel C. Paul, "Body Shop Founder Pushes Her Ideal Approach to Profit," *Christian Science Monitor*. March 5, 2001, p. 20.

12. Cole, "True Colours."

13. Ibid.

14. Anita Roddick. "Constructive Lunacy." anitaroddick.com. http://www.anitaroddick.com, November 3, 2001.

15. Martin Waller, "Anita Could Be Neater," *Times* (London). September 28, 2002, p. 51.

16. "Anita Roddick," *Across the Board*. January 2001, p. 15.

17. Ibid.

18. Hugh Chow, "Anita Gets Down to Business," *Straits Times* (Singapore). November 26, 2003.

19. Teena Lyons, "Body Shop Is Back—and Fitter than Ever," *Daily Mail* (United Kingdom). November 16, 2005.

20. "From Ethics to Elixirs: A Tale of the Market," *Toronto Star*. June 10, 2001, p. WB1.

21. Gordon Thomson, "Fury as Body Shop Founder 'Snubs' Staff," *Evening Times* (Glasgow). September 16, 2004, p. 29.

22. Anita Roddick. "A day in the Life of . . . Dame Anita Roddick." anitaroddick.com. http://www.anitaroddick.com, March 20, 2006.

23. Sean Poulter, "Body Shop Boycott Call over 640m 'Sellout' by Roddick," *Daily Mail* (London). March 18, 2006, p. 39.

24. Anita Roddick. "Be Brave, Be Different." anitaroddick.com. http://www.anitaroddick.com, June 12, 2006.

25. Nagano, "Cosmetic Crusader."

26. Chris Blackhurst, "There's a Word for All of This, Anita . . . and It's Hypocrisy," *Evening Standard*. May 15, 2006, p. 27.

27. Roddick. "A Day in the life."

28. Ibid.

29. Anita Roddick. "Hepatitis C and Me." anitaroddick.com. http://www.anitaroddick.com, February 14, 2007.

30. Ibid.

31. Gordon Roddick. "I Will Miss Her Every Day." anitaroddick.com. http://www.anitaroddick.com, October 16, 2007.

32. Robert Pagnamenta and Suzy Jagger, "Green Queen Who Inspired Millions," *Times* (London). September 11, 2007.

33. Ed Harris, "Roddick Given Green Send-off She Wanted," *Evening Standard*. September 25, 2007, p. 11.

34. "Don't Hang Up! Anita's Memorial." anitaroddick.com. http://www.anitaroddick.com, November 12, 2007.

35. Ibid.

36. Richard Gillis, "A Gift for Narrative and a Passion for Fair Trade," *Irish Times*. January 14, 2008.

BIBLIOGRAPHY

Alderson, Andrew. "Gordon Roddick: I Want to Do Anita Justice." *Sunday Telegraph*, October 21, 2007.

"Anita Roddick," *Across the Board*, January 2001.

"Anita Roddick—Business Thinkers and Management Giants." Bloomsbury Business Library (2007).

Barber, Lynn. "The Lynn Barber Interview: Fruitful Fidget." *The Independent* (London), March 3, 1991.

Beard, Matthew. "Anita Roddick Says Body Shop Has Become a 'Dysfunctional Coffin.'" *The Independent* (London), August 25, 2001.

Bennett, Catherine. "Look: Power of the Body Politic." *Sunday Times* (London), March 6, 1988.

Blackhurst, Chris. "There's a Word for All of This, Anita . . . and It's Hypocrisy." *Evening Standard*, May 15, 2006.

Boulter, Annette. "I Was Her First Shop Worker: She Was My Inspiration." *Times* (London), September 12, 2007.

Brabazon, Tara. "Buff Puffing an Empire: The Body Shop and Colonization by Other Means." *Journal of Media & Cultural Studies* 15:2 (2001).

Burlingham, Bo. "The Woman Has Changed Business Forever." Mansueto Ventures, June 1990.

Chapman, John. "Body Blow to Body Shop as Founder Anita Quits." *Sunday Express*, September 17, 2000.

Chatzky, Jean Sherman. "Changing the World." *Forbes*, March 2, 1992.

Chow, Hugh. "Anita Gets Down to Business." *Straits Times* (Singapore), November 26, 2003.

Cole, Susan G. "The True Colours of Anita Roddick." *Now Magazine* (Toronto), Spring 2001.

Cowe, Roger. "Body Blow." *Guardian* (London), May 13, 1998.

Crampton, Robert. "Out of Body Experience," *Times* (London), May 26, 2001.

Davies, Jessica. "Why Women Can't Have Power and Sexuality." *Daily Mail* (London), February 12, 1993.

Devine, Miranda. "Wrinkle Queen Bursts the Bubble of Hope." *Daily Telegraph*, October 23, 2000.

"Don't Hang Up! Anita's Memorial." anitaroddick.com, November 12, 2007. Available online. URL: http://www. anitaroddick.com.

Elliot, Stuart. "The Body Shop's Campaign Offers Reality, Not Miracles." *New York Times*, August 26, 1997.

Elmer-Dewitt, Phillip, and Elizabeth Lea. "Anita the Agitator." *Time*, January 25, 1993.

Entine, Jon. "Anita Roddick's Unfair Trade." *Mail on Sunday*, September 16, 2007.

———. "A Social and Environmental Audit of The Body Shop: Anita Roddick and the Question of Character." July 1996. Available online. URL: http://www.jonentine. com/the-body-shop.html.

"From Ethics to Elixirs: A Tale of the Market," *Toronto Star*, June 10, 2001.

Garfield, Simon. "Anita and a Case of Fruit and Nuts. . . ." *Daily Mail* (London), October 10, 1994.

Gillis, Richard. "A Gift for Narrative and a Passion for Fair Trade." *Irish Times*, January 14, 2008.

Harris, Ed. "Roddick Given Green Send-off She Wanted." *Evening Standard*, September 25, 2007.

Johnson, Lucy. "Husband's Vow to Keep the Flame of Dame Anita's Legacy Alive." *Sunday Express*, February 17, 2008.

"Leader as Social Advocate: Building the Business by Building Community." *Leader to Leader*, Summer 2000.

Lyons, Teena. "Body Shop Is Back—and Fitter than Ever." *Daily Mail*, November 16, 2005.

MacKenzie, Susie. "Women: Prophet and Gloss—Public Lives—Anita Roddick." *Guardian* (London), September 11, 1991.

Miles, Alice. "Roddick's Ruse: It Wasn't the Moisteriser After All." *Times* (London), September 12, 2007.

Miller, Russell. "Did the Green Goddess Sell Out?" *Daily Mail*, September 12, 2007.

Nagano, Miho. "She Was a Cosmetic Crusader." *Investor's Business Daily*, April 9, 2008.

Olins, Rufus. "Body Shop Goes for a New Shape." *Sunday Times* (London), June 1, 1997.

Pagnamenta, Robert, and Suzy Jagger. "Green Queen Who Inspired Millions." *Times* (London), September 11, 2007.

Paul, Noel C. "Body Shop Founder Pushes Her Ideal Approach to Profit." *Christian Science Monitor*, March 5, 2001.

"Pioneering Body Shop Founder Who Fought for Green Issues." *Irish Times*, September 15, 2007.

Pless, Nicola M. "Understanding Responsible Leadership: Role Identity and Motivational Drivers." *Journal of Business Ethics* 74, 2007.

Poulter, Sean. "Body Shop Boycott Call Over 640m 'Sell-out' by Roddick." *Daily Mail* (London), March 18, 2006.

Robb, Christina. "Whole-earth Beauty: Body Shop's Founder Trots the Globe in Quest of Effective—and Environmentally Safe—Cosmetic Products." *Boston Globe*, September 15, 1990.

Roddick, Anita. "Be Brave, Be Different," anitaroddick.com, Available online. URL: http://www.anitaroddick.com, June 12, 2006.

———. *Body and Soul*, New York: Crown Publishers, 1991.

———. *Business as Unusual*. London: Anita Roddick Publications, 2005.

———. "Constructive Lunacy," anitaroddick.com. Available online. URL: http://www.anitaroddick.com, November 3, 2001.

———. "A Day in the Life of . . . Dame Anita Roddick," anitaroddick.com. Available online. URL: http://www.anitaroddick.com, March 20, 2006.

———. "Diary, Anita Roddick." *New Statesman*, October 16, 2000.

———. "Hepatitis C and Me" anitaroddick.com. Available online. URL: http://www.anitaroddick.com, February 14, 2007.

Roddick, Gordon. "I Will Miss Her Every Day," anitaroddick.com. Available online. URL: http://www.anitaroddick.com, October 16, 2007.

Rushe, Dominic. "Body and Soul for Sale." *Sunday Times* (London), April 15, 2001.

Simpson, Anne. "Mother Nature." *Courier Mail* (Brisbane, Australia), October 28, 2000.

Stead, Deborah. "Managing: Secrets to a Cosmic Cosmetician." *New York Times*, September 23, 1990.

Thomson, Gordon. "Fury as Body Shop Founder 'Snubs' Staff." *Evening Times* (Glasgow), September 16, 2004.

Tooher, Patrick. "Roddick Falls Out with Oldest Friend." *The Independent* (London), October 1, 1995.

Vicenzi, Penny. "Labour and Love." *Times* (London), June 19, 1987.

Waller, Martin. "Anita Could Be Neater." *Times* (London), September 28, 2002.

Yeung, Linda. "Anita Roddick Takes the Global Point of View." *South China Morning Post*, November 30, 1997.

FURTHER RESOURCES

BOOKS

Roddick, Anita. *Body and Soul*. New York: Crown Publishers, 1991.

———. *Business as Ususual*. London: Anita Roddick Publications, 2000.

———. *A Revolution in Kindness*. London: Anita Roddick Publications, 2003.

WEB SITES

Anita Roddick's Official Web Site
http://www.anitaroddick.com

The Body Shop
http://www.thebodyshop.com

The Roddick Foundation
http://www.theroddickfoundation.com

PICTURE CREDITS

Page

9: David Levenson/Getty Images News/Getty Images

20: AP Images

24: © John Norman/Alamy

30: © Ange/Alamy

42: Keystone/Hulton Archive/Getty Images

48: ZUMA/Newscom

51: © Linda Kennedy/Alamy

58: Gillian Allen/AP Images

65: Press Association via AP Images

67: © Christopher Pillitz/Alamy

75: AFP Photos/Newscom

77: Eric Draper/AP Images

79: Jacques Brinon/AP Images

88: REUTERS/Kirsty Wigglesworth /Landov

95: Chris Jackson/Getty Images News/Getty Images

INDEX

A

acid rain 63
Afghanistan 78
Africa 11, 25–26, 76
  products found in 7–8
  Rhassoul mud from 37
  Wodaabe tribe in 71
almond oil 10, 38
aloe vera 10
Amchitka 61
Amnesty International 93
Amsterdam 61
Angola 3 Campaign 93
animal
  testing 13, 46, 49, 62, 76,
    89
  rights 44, 70, 75
Avon 85
Auschwitz 12
Australia 11, 26, 28–29, 52
awards 57, 79

B

Bath & Body Works
  competition 62, 73, 81
Bath, England 19
Beauty baskets 39, 41
Ben & Jerry's Ice Cream 59,
  72
Berkeley, California 30, 73
Biggs, Brooke Shelby 86
Big Issue, The (magazine) 13
Black Panthers 90
Blair, Tony 94
body scrubs 39
Body Shop, The 30, 94
  after 91–94
  bottles and jars 36, 39,
    45–46, 62
  catalog business 65
  color design of 19, 38–39,
    49, 55, 62, 63, 76
  concept for 36

corporate headquarters
  12–13, 48, 56, 63–64
customers 40, 52, 64, 66,
  71, 74, 81–83, 90
employees 12–15, 47, 52–
  53, 56, 63–64, 66, 71, 74,
  76, 84, 90
first store 10, 36, 38–39, 43,
  45, 54
founders 7, 9, 95
franchises 12–13, 43, 49,
  60, 71, 73, 76
labels 39
locations 8, 41–44, 47–48,
  52, 54, 57, 59–60, 62, 64,
  66, 70–73, 76, 81–82, 86,
  90
perfume bar in 40
posters in 13, 15, 52, 59–
  60, 62–64, 82, 84
production facility 8, 48, 55
products 8–11, 21, 28, 36–
  47, 49, 51–53, 58–59, 62,
  72–75, 81–84, 95–96
public sale of 54–57, 59, 65,
  75–76, 83
sale of 79–80, 82, 88–91
shareholders 57, 60, 67, 71,
  75–76, 83–85, 87–89
stories 8, 45, 50, 52–53, 62,
  74, 81, 96
success of 13, 15, 40, 42,
  44–46, 51–52, 55, 72, 74
Body Shop Foundation 70, 86
Body and Soul 26, 86
  environmental issues in 60
  family in 18
  looking for new products
    in 10
  Paddington's in 33
  teaching in 24
  travels in 45
Body and Soul Organization
  93

Boys Town in India 58
  wooden rollers from 11, 59
Brave Hearts, Rebel Spirits 86
Brazil 10, 59, 66, 74
Brighton, England
  first store in 38–39, 41
British Broadcasting Corporation (BBC) 55
Brussels, Belgium
  store in 43
Buenos Aires, Argentina 35, 38, 43
Bush, George H. W. 84
Business as Unusual 92
  social activism in 12
  travels in 29, 83
Business Ethics 73
Businesses for Social Responsibility 72
Business Woman of the Year award 57

C

Campaign for Freedom Against Hunger 19
Campaign for Nuclear Disarmament 19
capitalism 81
Chichester, England
  second store in 41
childhood 15–26
China, 76, 78
  products found in 7
cirrhosis 91
Clifton Café
  family business 16–20, 33
cocoa butter 10, 28, 30, 38, 45
community service 12
conservationism 70
Constantine, Mark 41–42
controversy
  and Anita's personality 13–15

coping the Berkeley store 30
  over business practices 73–75, 80, 82, 86
  social issues 72
cosmetics industry 89
  dislike of 10, 13, 37, 40, 44, 53, 64, 70, 76
Cosmopolitan 47
Cucumber Cleansing Mask 39
Cultural Survival 59
cultures
  learning about 10–14

D

Dadd, Debra Lynn 72
Daily Mail 74
Dean, James 19
death 92–95
deforestation 61
Denmark 48
Diana, Princess 65

E

ecological concern 9
education
  after high school 19–21
  elementary school 18–19
El Cubana
  family nightclub 20, 26–28, 33
elderflower eye gel 75
Elizabeth II, Queen of England 87
Entine, Jon 73
Entrepreneurial Champion Award 79
environment principles 9, 93, 95
  and The Body Shop 7, 46, 53, 56–57, 63–64, 66, 70–73, 79, 81, 92
Estée Lauder 60
Evening Argus newspaper 39

F

fair trade 53, 85, 95
family
    Italian immigrants 15–17
Finland 48
Forbes 62
free trade 49
Friends of the Earth 60, 93

G

global concern
    and The Body Shop 7, 13
Great Britain 17
    businesses 15, 76, 81, 94
Greece 24
Greenpeace 13, 59–61
Guildhall School for Music and
    Drama 19

H

Harlem Community Giving
    Program 78
Have a Heart campaign 72
Hepatitis C trust 91, 93
herbalists 10, 37–38, 41–42
Hippie Trail 25–26
Holland 48, 77
Holocaust 12, 19
honey and beeswax cleanser 41
Honey and Oatmeal Scrub
    Mask 39
honey shampoos 45
humanitarian 11, 49, 63
human rights
    passion for 44, 46–47, 49–
    50, 52, 70, 77, 85, 92–93
Human Rights Watch 77–78
Hurricane Katrina 90, 93

I

Iceland 48
Independent, The (newspaper)
    7, 15, 73

India 59, 71, 76
    poverty in 11
Indonesia
    rain forest 61
International Herald Tribune 22
International Labour Organi-
    zation 24
Israel 10
    kibbutz in 21–23
Italy 17, 29

J

Japan 58
jojoba oil 38
Judaism 21
Juice It gel products 82

K

Kibbutz 21–23

L

Limited, The 62
Littlehampton, England
    growing up in 8, 16
    living in 11, 23–24, 26–29,
    33, 38, 55, 90
    teaching in 23–24
London, England 7–8, 29, 90
    corporate offices in 63–64
    protests in 66
    store in 47
London's National Theatre
    94
London School of Economics
    85–86
London Stock Exchange 55–
    57, 76
L'Oréal 89–90
lotions
    lettuce 41–42
    selling 8, 28, 30, 36, 38–43,
    45, 49, 51, 74–75, 82, 95
Love your body campaign 76

M

Mandela, Nelson 26
mango butter 74
Maude Allen Secondary Modern 19, 23
McGlinn, Ian 41, 83
media attention 47, 49–50, 53, 90
Mexico
    Nanhu Indians of 73
Ms magazine 80

N

Nader, Ralph 80
National Jewish Fund 22
National Labor Committee 93
natural products
    selling 8–10, 37–39, 44, 47, 49, 59
Naturewatch 89
Nepal 8, 10, 59
Netherlands 61
Newton Park College of Education 19–21
New York City 35, 64–65, 77–78
    stores in 13–14
New York Post 86
New York Stock Exchange 57
North Sea
    hazardous waste in 59–60

O

Obama, Barack 61
Origins 60
Owen-Jones, Lindsey 89

P

Paddington's restaurant 32–35
Palm Shine shampoo 82
Panama Canal 25
Paris 21–22

Peppermint Foot Lotion 47, 75
Perilli, Bruno (brother) 17
Perilli, Donny 17
Perilli, Gilda (mother) 17, 21, 29, 31, 47, 70, 90
    babysitting 33–34, 40
    businesses 18–20, 26–28, 33
Perilli, Henry (father)
    death 17–18
Perilli, Lydia (sister) 17
Perilli, Velia (sister) 17
Persian Gulf War 72
personality
    charming 14, 32
    creativity 8, 40
    fidgety 8, 14
    principles 9, 13
    strong work ethic 15, 40, 42
    talker 14–15, 28
protests 66, 86
    against acid rain 13
    against animal testing 13
    early 19
    extreme 61
public relations 47, 55, 76

Q

Quaker principles
    in business 43–44, 71

R

Rainforest Action Network 93
rainforest issues 15, 64, 66
Reno, Nevada 31
Reprieve 91–93
Revolution of Kindness, A 86
Roddick Foundation 91–93
Roddick, Gordon (husband) 13, 93–94
    affair 82
    businesses 31–34, 37, 47–48, 54–55, 69, 74, 76, 79–80, 82–83, 86–87, 89

childhood dream 35
family 29
horse trip 35–36, 38, 43
marriage 31
meeting 27–28
personality 32–33
Roddick, Justine (daughter)
29, 31, 33–34, 36, 38, 40, 47,
69, 84, 93–94
Roddick, Samantha (daughter)
31, 33–34, 36, 38, 40, 47, 69,
84, 90–91, 93–94
Romania 65
Ruby doll 76

S

San Francisco
travels to 29–30
Saunders, Peter 87
Save the Whales 13, 15, 60
Scotland 83–84, 89
Seaweed and Birch Shampoo
39
segregation laws 25–26
September 11, 2001 terrorist
attacks 86
Shelter and Freedom from
Hunger 19
Soapworks factory 84, 89
social activism 96
issues 9–10, 12–14, 19,
43, 50, 53, 62–63, 65, 67,
70, 72, 76, 81, 83, 85–87,
90–91
local issues 33
St. Catherine's Convent 18–19
Stride Rite 72
St. Winifred's hotel 31–32, 36
Switzerland
United Nations in 10,
24–25

T

Tahiti

products found in 10–11,
26, 28, 44–45
tea tree oil 52
Tobacco Flower cosmetics 82
Toronto Star 89
travels 29, 77, 83, 86, 96
early 10–11, 21, 25, 45
products found during 7–8,
10, 28, 44–45, 49, 58–59,
70–71, 74

U

United Nations 64
climate summit 61
working in 10, 24–25
United States 59, 61, 65, 78,
86
labor unions 60
stores in 60, 62, 72, 81–83,
85
travels to 29–31
Unrepresented People and
Nations 77
U.S. Coast Guard 61
U.S. Drug Enforcement
Agency 82

V

Vienna 10
Vogue 70

W

water hyacinths
paper from 9
Whitman, Walt
Leaves of Grass 94
World Trade Organisation to
the Nigerian Ogoni people
46
World Trade Organization 77

Y

Yanomami Indians 66

ABOUT THE AUTHOR

SHERRY BECK PAPROCKI is a freelance journalist and author who has written eight juvenile biographies for Chelsea House. *Oprah Winfrey* (2006) earned a spot on the 2006 Nonfiction Honor List created by the Voice of Youth Advocates (VOYA). In addition, she has written *Bob Marley* (2006), *Vicente Fox* (2002), *Martha Stewart* (2008), *Ellen DeGeneres* (2008), *Princess Diana* (2008), *Katie Couric* (2001), and *Michelle Kwan* (2001). Her bylines have appeared in *Principal* magazine, *Preservation* magazine, *The Chicago Tribune*, the *Cleveland Plain Dealer*, and many others. She is a graduate of The Ohio State University School of Journalism and resides near Columbus, Ohio, where she also serves as an adjunct faculty member of Otterbein College. She and her husband, Ray, are the parents of two adult children, Justin and Ana Paprocki.